BTEC Level 2 First Study Skills Guide in Business

Welcome to your Study Skills Guide! You can make it your own – start by adding your personal and course details below...

Student's name: ____________________

BTEC course title: ____________________

Date started: ____________________

Mandatory units:

____

____

____

Optional units:

____

____

____

____

Centre name: ____________________

Centre address:

____

____

____

Tutor's name: ____________________

Published by Pearson Education Limited, a company incorporated in England and Wales, having its registered office at Edinburgh Gate, Harlow, Essex, CM20 2JE. Registered company number: 872828

Edexcel is a registered trademark of Edexcel Limited

First published 2010

13
12

British Library Cataloguing in Publication Data
A catalogue record for this book is available from the British Library

ISBN 978 1 84690 578 0

Typeset and edited by Ken Vail Graphic Design
Cover design by Visual Philosophy, created by EMC Design
Cover photo/illustration © Image Source Ltd: Nigel Riches
Printed in Great Britain by Ashford Colour Press Ltd., Gosport, Hampshire

Acknowledgements
The author and publisher would like to thank the following individuals and organisations for permission to reproduce photographs:
Alamy Images: ACE STOCK LIMITED 56, Keith Morris 76, Jacky Chapman, Janine Wiedel Photolibrary 13; **Corbis:** 62, Comstock 4; **Getty Images:** Michael Rosenfeld 36; **iStockphoto:** Rene Mansi 14; **Pearson Education Ltd:** Steve Shott 24, Ian Wedgewood 34; **Photolibrary.com:** Eric Audras 40; **SuperStock:** View Pictures Ltd 74; **TopFoto:** John Powell 20

Cover images: *Front:* **Image Source Ltd:** Nigel Riches

All other images © Pearson Education

Every effort has been made to contact copyright holders of material reproduced in this book. Any omissions will be rectified in subsequent printings if notice is given to the publishers.

Websites
Go to www.pearsonhotlinks.co.uk to gain access to relevant website links and information on how they can aid your studies. When you access the site, search for either the express code 5780S, title BTEC Level 2 First Study Skills Guide in Business or ISBN 9781846905780.

Contents

Popular progression pathways

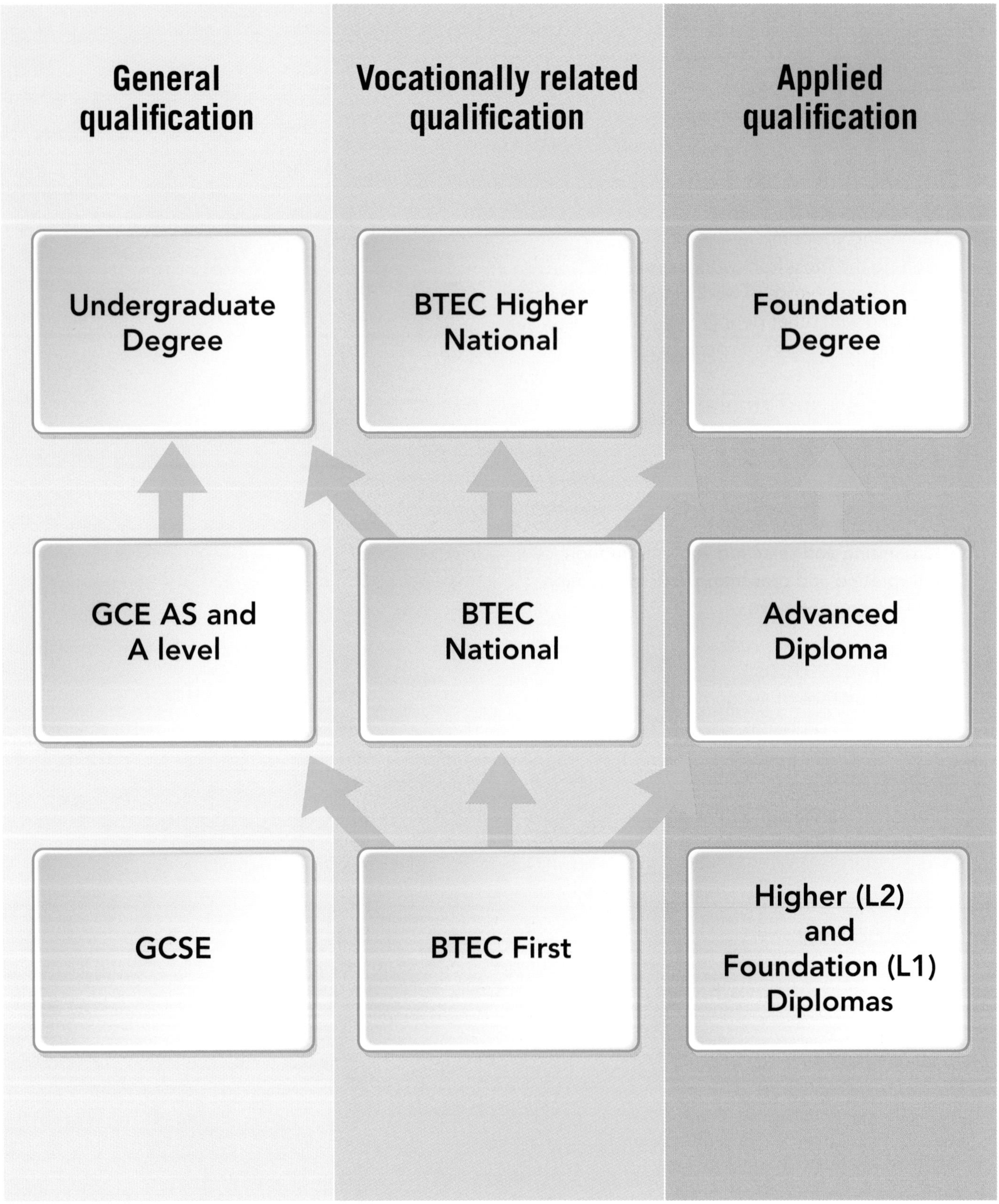

General qualification	Vocationally related qualification	Applied qualification
Undergraduate Degree	BTEC Higher National	Foundation Degree
GCE AS and A level	BTEC National	Advanced Diploma
GCSE	BTEC First	Higher (L2) and Foundation (L1) Diplomas

Your BTEC First course

Early days

Every year many new learners start BTEC Level 2 First courses, enjoy the challenge and successfully achieve their award. Some do this the easy way; others make it harder for themselves.

Everyone will have different feelings when they start their course.

Case study: Thinking positively

Before Nadia commenced her BTEC First in Business she was nervous about whether she would cope with the demands of the course. In general, she finds it difficult to be confident about new adventures and tends to dwell on the down side of things.

'I often concentrate on the negatives, especially when it comes to my studies. I sometimes think that I'm not much good at studying and, in the past, have wondered whether I should leave school as soon as possible.

During the induction week of the BTEC First in Business, the tutors set us various activities to help us all get to know the course and each other. One of these activities was about the power of positive thinking. We were taught to alter our negative thoughts and turn them into positive ones, and to keep doing this until our minds do it automatically.

For example, before starting the course, if I was given an assignment, immediately I would think that I could not do it. This made me frightened and frustrated. After trying the activity, I began telling myself that I am good at assignments. I kept repeating this to myself over a period of time and have gradually become more confident.

I am now achieving at a much higher level than I ever thought possible and I apply this way of thinking to other aspects of my life.'

About your course

What do you know already?

If someone asks you about your course, could you give a short, accurate description? If you can, you have a good understanding of what your course is about. This has several benefits.

Four benefits of understanding your course

1 You will be better prepared and organised.

2 You can make links between the course and the world around you.

3 You can check how your personal interests and hobbies relate to the course.

4 You will be alert to information that relates to topics you are studying, whether it's from conversations with family and friends, watching television or at a part-time job.

Read any information you have been given by your centre. You can also check the Edexcel website for further details – www.edexcel.com.

TOP TIP

If you have a part-time job, you're likely to be involved in helping customers and colleagues. These are important skills for any BTEC First learner.

TRY THIS

Write down your interests and hobbies and identify those that relate to your studies in any way.

Interest/hobby	How this relates to my studies

What else do you need to know?

Five facts you should find out about your course

1. The type of BTEC qualification you are studying.
2. How many credits your qualification is worth.
3. The number of mandatory units you will study and what they cover.
4. How many credits the mandatory units are worth.
5. The number of optional units you need to study in total and the options available in your centre.

Case study: Fitting it all together

When Gareth started the BTEC First in Business, even though there was a comprehensive induction programme, he found it difficult to see how the different units of his course fitted together to reflect the way a business operates.

Similarly, he thought that functional skills and personal, learning and thinking skills (PLTS) were separate from the main programme and questioned why he needed to study these as they seemed irrelevant.

Two months later, he is gradually beginning to see how the course units all fit together and the extra skills he is gaining mean he can complete his assignments.

A period of work experience has reaffirmed for Gareth how the different units complement one another and has shown him that, in a real business, production, marketing, human resources, finance, sales and customer service all work together to make the company successful.

'I now understand what the course is trying to do. It gives me the important skills that I need to work in any business or management function and lets me practise them. I need to have good research, problem-solving and teamworking skills, as well as be able to communicate properly, use ICT and undertake numerical calculations.'

BTEC FACT

BTEC First Certificate = 15 credits

BTEC First Extended Certificate = 30 credits

BTEC First Diploma = 60 credits

Generally, the more credits there are, the longer it takes to study for the qualification.

TRY THIS

Find out which optional units your centre offers. To check the topics covered in each unit go to www.pearsonhotlinks.co.uk, insert the express code 5780S and click on the link for this page.

TOP TIP

If you have a choice of optional units in your centre and are struggling to decide, talk through your ideas with your tutor.

Activity: How well do you know your course?

Complete this activity to check that you know the main facts. Compare your answers with a friend. You should have similar answers except where you make personal choices, such as about optional units. Your tutor can help you complete number 9.

1 The correct title of the BTEC award I am studying is:

2 The length of time it will take me to complete my award is:

3 The number of mandatory units I have to study is:

4 The titles of my mandatory units, and their credit values, are:

5 The main topics I will learn in each mandatory unit include:

Mandatory unit	Main topics

6 The number of credits I need to achieve by studying optional units is:

7 The titles of my optional units, and their credit values, are:

8 The main topics I will learn in each optional unit include:

Optional unit	Main topics

9 Other important aspects of my course are:

10 After I have achieved my BTEC First, my options include:

Introduction to the business sector

The Business Sector covers a vast range of occupations and professions. A BTEC First in Business is the ideal qualification to give you an awareness of the variety of interesting opportunities that are available.

During your BTEC First in Business, you will learn about the reasons why particular businesses exist: some businesses make or sell a product and some provide a service; some exist to make a profit and some do not. From here, you will go on to explore the variety of different types of business organisation, from the large multinational companies such as Amazon, to the small businesses owned and run by just one person.

All businesses rely on money to allow them to operate. The course will show how a business raises money and how it monitors its performance through accurate financial forecasting.

Of course, all of the different activities that take place in business organisations require people to make them happen. An important part of the BTEC First in Business is for you to learn about the various roles that people perform, and how employees are recruited and trained for these positions.

The BTEC First includes numerous optional units covering specialist areas such as communicating effectively within organisations; training and developing people; the importance of customer service; consumer rights; conducting business on the internet; and personal-selling skills. The unit on how to start a small business covers the skills and knowledge required to set up a company, from having that all-important idea, through how to raise finance, to planning to reduce the risk of failure.

The BTEC First in Business is valued by employers and can be a route to employment or to a higher level Business Studies programme. If you decide to go straight into employment, you might obtain a trainee position. Trainee positions may be available in finance and general administration, sales and marketing, retailing, warehousing and distribution, insurance, general management and personnel administration.

If you use your BTEC First to progress on to a BTEC Level 3 National Diploma in Business, possibly followed by a degree, a range of professions and occupations could be open to you. Those who gain higher and professional qualifications in business and business-related subjects, such as accountancy, marketing, personnel and banking, may progress into one the jobs listed below. This is just a small sample of the sorts of opportunities that could be available:

- accountant
- advertising account executive
- banker (retail/investment/commercial)
- building society manager
- buyer (industrial/retail)
- company secretary
- commodity or futures broker
- distribution or logistics manager
- insurance underwriter
- management consultant
- marketing executive
- market research executive
- human resources manager
- public relations account executive
- recruitment consultant
- retail manager
- sales executive
- stockbroker.

The contribution that businesses make to the UK economy is significant. Businesses employ people and, in return for their work and expertise, pay wages or salaries. Both employees and the businesses themselves pay taxes to the government. The UK government uses the money collected in taxes to provide a range of services, such as schools, roads, the National Health Service, the Armed Forces and so on.

It is easy to imagine what would happen if there were fewer businesses – fewer people would be able to work, more people would claim unemployment benefit, and the government would get less money from taxes. It would still have to provide all the services we are used to and pay for the increased level of unemployment benefit claims. So, the Business Sector is clearly vital to the wellbeing of a country and its people.

The following case study highlights how the skills that you will learn on the BTEC First can help you to achieve your career goals.

Case study: Introduction to your sector

David is 16 and is currently completing a BTEC First in Business at his local comprehensive school. David likes practical activities and project work, and for these reasons he was drawn to the BTEC First course. The programme includes the study of the role of people in organisations and David has a particular interest in this area.

He is currently on a two-week work experience placement and, with the help of his teacher and the school careers adviser, he has been fortunate enough to be placed in the human resource office of a large hotel and private health and fitness centre. The assistant human resource manager has been assigned to look after him. She will ensure that David receives a broad experience, giving him a taste of what a human resource department does. David has been surprised to find out how many roles exist within the HR department, including administration, training and development, and recruitment and selection.

David's work experience has been well structured so that he is able to use the skills he has developed on the BTEC First.

On Monday he worked in the training department and was asked to create a spreadsheet to record the names of the staff in the health and fitness centre and the training they have undertaken during the last 12 months. David enjoyed this task, as he was able to be creative in the way the spreadsheet was designed. Tomorrow, David has been asked to sit in as an observer on a number of recruitment interviews for the post of gymnasium manager.

'I am thoroughly enjoying this experience as it allows me to practise the skills I have learnt and it is giving me an opportunity to gather evidence for my People in Organisations assignment. Next week I will be helping one of the company's trainers to devise a course for administrative personnel on how to create simple spreadsheets.

The company employs over 300 people and, therefore, is important to the local economy. I am hoping that, if I perform well during my work experience, there may be an opportunity to join the company as a trainee in human resource administration when I finish my BTEC First in Business.'

Skills you need for your sector

Here are some examples of the transferable skills that you could develop as a result of studying the BTEC First in Business. Employers' job vacancy details often refer to them when they advertise for staff. You can mention these skills on your CV to demonstrate the broad range of qualities you have to offer.

Analysing and selecting information

When collecting evidence for your assignments, you may have to select information to use in your work and make sense of what it is saying. These are important skills that employers look for in potential employees.

Communicating effectively

Throughout your course, you will develop skills in both written and non-written methods of communication. Employers are always keen to hire people who are good communicators, cutting down on mistakes caused by misunderstandings between different parts of the business.

Your BTEC course will help you develop all-round skills, like communication.

Teamwork

Much of what goes on in business involves the ability to work well in teams and for teams to work together to solve problems. The BTEC First in Business encourages all learners to work together in teams in order to achieve group and individual goals.

Understanding and interpreting numerical data

Whatever job you perform in a business, there will be occasions when you have to understand and interpret numerical data. This could mean analysing a simple bar chart or line graph, or performing calculations. Again, all employers need people who can demonstrate these skills.

Problem solving

Employers want people who know how to solve problems for themselves and within teams. If employees always rely on their managers to solve problems, the flow of work through the business slows up as a result. Employers want people who show initiative and who can make recommendations for solving problems.

TOP TIP

Take time to identify the skills you already possess and are good at, and those that need more work. Be honest with yourself. If you struggle with analysing data, for example, talk to your tutor about getting some extra help in this area.

Computer literacy

Few jobs these days require no computer knowledge. Increasingly, employers want staff that can use basic and, sometimes, more advanced computer applications. The BTEC First course in Business contains opportunities to practise your IT skills using Word, Excel, the internet and email.

Computer literacy is essential in Business. If you are struggling with your computer skills, don't be afraid to seek extra help.

Meeting deadlines

All businesses have objectives that have to be met. In order to meet these objectives, deadlines have to be set at every level of the business. The BTEC First course, with its scheduled programme of assignments, will teach you the importance of meeting deadlines. If you miss assignment deadlines, you run the risk of not achieving the qualification. Similarly, in business, if you consistently fail to meet deadlines, you may not be successful.

Organising your time and prioritising your work

Being able to manage your time is critical when working in the Business Sector. Sometimes it is difficult to work out which of the many tasks that you have to do is the most important. Sometimes, people try to do too many things at once and are not successful at any of them, causing stress and confusion. Through tutorials, your tutor will help you to manage your time effectively and will assist you in prioritising the various tasks that you have to perform.

Writing reports

At some point in your working life, you will probably have to produce a report. All businesses rely on reports in order to inform people inside and outside the organisation. The BTEC First in Business will teach you how to structure, write and produce business reports.

In addition to the skills outlined above, research has shown that employers require employees to possess certain other skill sets. In BTEC programmes, these are grouped together and described as personal, learning and thinking skills (PLTS) and functional skills. These skills will be developed throughout the course and are discussed further in this Study Skills Guide (see page 81).

More about BTEC Level 2 Firsts

What is different about a BTEC Level 2 First?

How you learn

Expect to be 'hands-on'. BTEC Level 2 Firsts are practical and focus on the skills and knowledge needed in the workplace. You will learn new things and learn how to apply your knowledge.

BTEC First learners are expected to take responsibility for their own learning and be keen and well-organised. You should enjoy having more freedom, while knowing you can still ask for help or support if you need it.

How you are assessed

Many BTEC First courses are completed in one year, but if you are taking GCSEs as well, you may be doing it over two years or more. You will be assessed by completing **assignments** written by your tutors. These are based on **learning outcomes** set by Edexcel. Each assignment will have a deadline.

TOP TIP

You can use your Study Skills Guide with the Edexcel Student Book for BTEC Level 2 First Business (Edexcel, 2010). It includes the main knowledge you'll need, with tips from BTEC experts, Edexcel assignment tips, assessment activities and up-to-date case studies from industry experts, plus handy references to your Study Skills Guide.

BTEC FACT

On a BTEC course you achieve individual criteria at pass, merit or distinction for your assignments. You will receive a pass, merit or distinction **grade** for completed units and then one of these three grades for the whole course.

Case study: Some reasons for choosing a BTEC First in Business

When Joel received his GCSE results, he decided that he wanted to do an applied course which related to the real world. He had always liked projects that involved some investigation and reporting back on the findings.

'I think following a BTEC programme is a very exciting way to study. It has given me the knowledge, skills and understanding that I will need in the world of work. I particularly like the activities, which are done individually, in small groups or as a whole class. All the units on the BTEC First in Business are related to the business world and can be applied to real-life situations – such as to small local businesses, an area that really interests me.'

Joel is assessed through assignments, which are marked by his tutor. These can be graded fail, pass, merit or distinction. Joel enjoys the learner-centred teaching on the course, meaning that responsibility for learning rests with him. This allows Joel to explore areas in different ways and to come up with his own conclusions about what has been taught and discussed.

Joel loves the degree of independence given to the learners on the course and feels that the BTEC approach really suits him.

Getting the most from your BTEC

Getting the most from your BTEC involves several skills, such as using your time effectively and working well with other people. Knowing yourself is also important.

Knowing yourself

How would you describe yourself? Make some notes here.

If you described yourself to someone else, would you be able to sum up your temperament and personality, identify your strengths and weaknesses and list your skills? If not, is it because you've never thought about it or because you honestly don't have a clue?

Learning about yourself is often called self-analysis. You may have already done personality tests or careers profiles. If not, there are many available online. However, the information you gain from these profiles is useless unless you can apply it to what you are doing.

Your personality

Everyone is different. For example, some people:

- like to plan in advance; others prefer to be spontaneous
- love being part of a group; others prefer one or two close friends
- enjoy being the life and soul of the party; others prefer to sit quietly and feel uncomfortable at large social gatherings
- are imaginative and creative; others prefer to deal only with facts
- think carefully about all their options before making a decision; others follow their 'gut instincts' and often let their heart rule their head.

Case study: Personality questionnaire

During her BTEC First induction week, Ceri assesses her own personality through a questionnaire test. The results indicate that she is someone who likes to prepare for things well in advance and that she tends to be loyal to a small number of close friends, rather than having a desire to be part of a larger group. They also suggest that she is a relatively quiet person who likes to stay in the background, but that she is good at coming up with ideas and solutions to problems.

'It was very interesting to see the results of my personality test and, broadly, I agree with the findings. This has made me think about my future career options and I feel that, because of my personality type, there are some jobs that really wouldn't suit me. For example, I couldn't consider being in sales, as I am too quiet and reserved for this type of role. I think I will be more suited to a behind-the-scenes job, where I can work steadily to a good standard, such as a marketing administrator in a large company.'

TRY THIS 

Imagine one of your friends is describing your best features. What would they say?

Personalities in the workplace

There's a mix of personalities in most workplaces. Some people prefer to work behind the scenes, such as many IT practitioners, who like to concentrate on tasks they enjoy doing. Others love high-profile jobs, where they may often be involved in high-pressure situations, such as paramedics and television presenters. Most people fall somewhere between these two extremes.

In any job there will be some aspects that are more appealing and interesting than others. If you have a part-time job you will already know this. The same thing applies to any course you take!

Your personality and your BTEC First course

Understanding your personality means you can identify which parts of your course you are likely to find easy and which more difficult. Working out the aspects you need to develop should be positive. You can also think about how your strengths and weaknesses may affect other people.

- Natural planners find it easier to schedule work for assignments.
- Extroverts like giving presentations and working with others but may overwhelm quieter team members.
- Introverts often prefer to work alone and may be excellent at researching information.

BTEC FACT

All BTEC First courses enable you to develop your personal, learning and thinking skills (**PLTS**), which will help you to meet new challenges more easily. (See page 81.)

Activity: What is your personality type?

1a) Identify your own personality type, either by referring to a personality test you have done recently or by going online and doing a reliable test. Go to www.pearsonhotlinks.co.uk, insert the express code 5780S and click on the link for this activity.

Print a summary of the completed test or write a brief description of the results for future reference.

b) Use this information to identify the tasks and personal characteristics that you find easy or difficult.

	Easy	Difficult
Being punctual		
Planning how to do a job		
Working neatly and accurately		
Being well organised		
Having good ideas		
Taking on new challenges		
Being observant		
Working with details		
Being patient		
Coping with criticism		
Dealing with customers		
Making decisions		
Keeping calm under stress		
Using your own initiative		

	Easy	Difficult
Researching facts carefully and accurately		
Solving problems		
Meeting deadlines		
Finding and correcting own errors		
Clearing up after yourself		
Helping other people		
Working as a member of a team		
Being sensitive to the needs of others		
Respecting other people's opinions		
Being tactful and discreet		
Being even-tempered		

2 Which thing from your 'difficult' list do you think you should work on improving first? Start by identifying the benefits you will gain. Then decide how to achieve your goal.

TOP TIP

The more you understand your own personality, the easier it is to build on your strengths and compensate for your weaknesses.

Your knowledge and skills

You already have a great deal of knowledge, as well as practical and personal skills gained at school, at home and at work (if you have a part-time job). Now you need to assess these to identify your strengths and weaknesses.

To do this accurately, try to identify evidence for your knowledge and skills. Obvious examples are:

- previous qualifications
- school reports
- occasions when you have demonstrated particular skills, such as communicating with customers or colleagues in a part-time job.

Part-time jobs give you knowledge and skills in a real work setting.

Activity: Check your skills

1 Score yourself from 1 to 5 for each of the skills in the table opposite.

1 = I'm very good at this skill.

2 = I'm good but could improve this skill.

3 = This skill is only average and I know that I need to improve it.

4 = I'm weak at this skill and must work hard to improve it.

5 = I've never had the chance to develop this skill.

Enter the score in the column headed 'Score A' and add today's date.

2 Look back at the units and topics you will be studying for your course – you entered them into the chart on page 8–10. Use this to identify any additional skills that you know are important for your course and add them to the table. Then score yourself for these skills, too.

3 Identify the main skills you will need in order to be successful in your chosen career, and highlight them in the table.

Go back and score yourself against each skill after three, six and nine months. That way you can monitor your progress and check where you need to take action to develop the most important skills you will need.

English and communication skills	Score A (today) Date:	Score B (after three months) Date:	Score C (after six months) Date:	Score D (after nine months) Date:
Reading and understanding different types of texts and information				
Speaking to other people face to face				
Speaking clearly on the telephone				
Listening carefully				
Writing clearly and concisely				
Presenting information in a logical order				
Summarising information				
Using correct punctuation and spelling				
Joining in a group discussion				
Expressing your own ideas and opinions appropriately				
Persuading other people to do something				
Making an oral presentation and presenting ideas clearly				
ICT skills	**Score A** (today) Date:	**Score B** (after three months) Date:	**Score C** (after six months) Date:	**Score D** (after nine months) Date:
Using ICT equipment correctly and safely				
Using a range of software				
Accurate keyboarding				
Proofreading				
Using the internet to find and select appropriate information				
Using ICT equipment to communicate and exchange information				
Producing professional documents which include tables and graphics				
Creating and interpreting spreadsheets				
Using PowerPoint				

Maths and numeracy skills	**Score A** (today) Date:	**Score B** (after three months) Date:	**Score C** (after six months) Date:	**Score D** (after nine months) Date:
Carrying out calculations (eg money, time, measurements, etc) in a work-related situation				
Estimating amounts				
Understanding and interpreting data in tables, graphs, diagrams and charts				
Comparing prices and identifying best value for money				
Solving routine and non-routine work-related numerical problems				

Case study: Skills development

Terri is enjoying her BTEC First course in Business, particularly the way the course is designed to allow her to develop lots of additional skills, as well as learning about the world of business.

'I have found that, since being on the course, I am more confident at speaking to people face to face and I listen more carefully to what is being said. I am contributing to class discussions, which a year ago I don't think I would have been able to do. Now, I can even stand up and give a presentation, which previously would have filled me with dread.

During my work experience in a customer services department, I had to interview a customer, take details of their complaint and inform them how the problem would be resolved. I do not think I would have been able to do this without the confidence gained through studying on the course.

My numeracy skills are improving, but I still find this area quite difficult and I have a lot of work to do to get to the level I need. I am struggling particularly with interpreting graphs and doing calculations. My individual learning plan (ILP) has highlighted these as areas of weakness that my tutor will help me address, and we have set targets for my understanding over the coming months. In IT, I am not very good at producing spreadsheets, so my ILP will target this skill as well.

My career aim is to work in marketing and I know that I will have to produce graphs, carry out numerical calculations and use spreadsheets, so it is very important that I work hard to improve my skills. In the first five months of the course, I have already improved greatly in these skill areas and am looking forward to moving to the next level.'

Managing your time

Some people are brilliant at managing their time. They do everything they need to and have time left over for activities they enjoy. Other people complain that they don't know where the time goes.

Which are you? If you need help to manage your time – and most people do – you will find help here.

Why time management is important

- It means you stay in control, get less stressed and don't skip important tasks.
- Some weeks will be peaceful, others will be hectic.
- The amount of homework and assignments you have to do will vary.
- As deadlines approach, time always seems to go faster.
- Some work will need to be done quickly, maybe for the next lesson; other tasks may need to be done over several days or weeks. This needs careful planning.
- You may have several assignments or tasks to complete in a short space of time.
- You want to have a social life.

Avoiding time-wasting

We can all plan to do work, and then find our plans go wrong. There may be several reasons for this. How many of the following do *you* do?

Top time-wasting activities

1. Allowing (or encouraging) people to interrupt you.
2. Not having the information, handouts or textbook you need because you've lost them or lent them to someone else.
3. Chatting to people, making calls or sending texts when you should be working.
4. Getting distracted because you simply must keep checking out MySpace, Facebook or emails.
5. Putting off jobs until they are a total nightmare, then panicking.
6. Daydreaming.
7. Making a mess of something so you have to start all over again.

Planning and getting organised

The first step in managing your time is to plan ahead and be well organised. Some people are naturally good at this. They think ahead, write down their commitments in a diary or planner, and store their notes and handouts neatly and carefully so they can find them quickly.

How good are your working habits?

Talking to friends can take up a lot of time.

Improving your planning and organisational skills

1. Use a diary or planner to schedule working times into your weekdays and weekends.
2. Have a place for everything and everything in its place.
3. Be strict with yourself when you start work. If you aren't really in the mood, set a shorter time limit and give yourself a reward when the time is up.
4. Keep a diary in which you write down exactly what work you have to do.
5. Divide up long or complex tasks into manageable chunks and put each 'chunk' in your diary with a deadline of its own.
6. Write a 'to do' list if you have several different tasks. Tick them off as you go.
7. Always allow more time than you think you need for a task.

TRY THIS

Analyse your average day.

How many hours do you spend sleeping, eating, travelling, attending school or college, working and taking part in leisure activities?

How much time is left for homework and assignments?

Case study: Time management

Lewis has been studying on the BTEC First for three months and has had particular difficulty organising his time.

'My biggest problem was recognising time-wasters. I didn't realise that friends – calling at the house when I'm studying and 'phoning my mobile – could be so disruptive. I used to welcome these interruptions as I enjoyed being with and talking to my friends.

After a while, I realised that I was not getting on with my work and that all these interruptions were really eating into my study time. On the BTEC First course you have to prioritise tasks in order to get them done and I learned that time-wasters get in the way of priorities! I now try to keep my BTEC study time and my personal life separate.

Two other problems that wasted my time were the lack of a plan and poor organisation. If you have a plan in place and carry it out in an organised way, then your chances of success are much greater. If I hadn't seen the impact my poor time management was having on my work, then I think I would have been in deep trouble by now and heading for failure. Thankfully, I got to grips with these issues early enough to do something about them.

I now work on Saturdays in an administrative role at a local cash and carry warehouse. It is very busy and there are lots of people who want to talk to me about all sorts of things that are unrelated to my work. Having learnt about time-wasters on the BTEC First, I tell them politely that I have to carry on with my work and will look forward to catching up with them during break time.'

TOP TIP

If you become distracted by social networking sites or email when you're working, set yourself a time limit of 10 minutes or so to indulge yourself.

BTEC FACT

If you have serious problems that are interfering with your ability to work or to concentrate, talk to your tutor. There are many ways in which BTEC learners who have personal difficulties can be supported to help them continue with their studies.

Activity: Managing time

1 The correct term for something you do in preference to starting a particular task is a 'displacement activity'. In the workplace this includes things like often going to the water cooler to get a drink, and constantly checking emails and so on online. People who work from home may tidy up, watch television or even cook a meal to put off starting a job.

Write down *your* top three displacement activities.

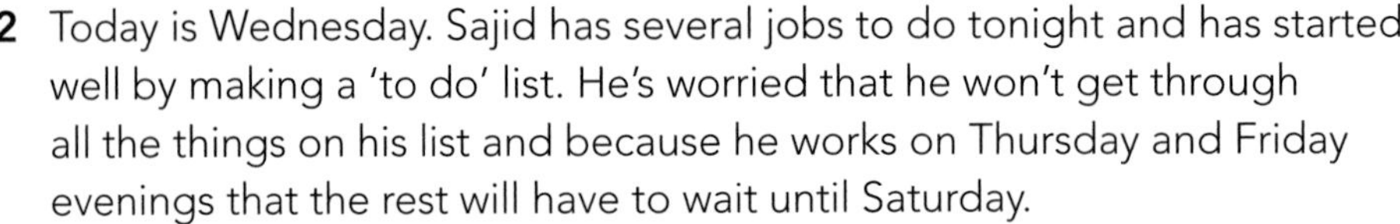

2 Today is Wednesday. Sajid has several jobs to do tonight and has started well by making a 'to do' list. He's worried that he won't get through all the things on his list and because he works on Thursday and Friday evenings that the rest will have to wait until Saturday.

a) Look through Sajid's list and decide which jobs are top priority and *must* be done tonight and which can be left until Saturday if he runs out of time.

b) Sajid is finding that his job is starting to interfere with his ability to do his assignments. What solutions can you suggest to help him?

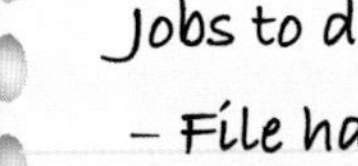

Jobs to do

- File handouts from today's classes
- Phone Tom (left early today) to tell him the time of our presentation tomorrow has been changed to 11 am
- Research information online for next Tuesday's lesson
- Complete table from rough notes in class today
- Rewrite section of leaflet to talk about at tutorial tomorrow
- Write out class's ideas for the charity of the year, ready for course representatives meeting tomorrow lunchtime
- Redo handout Tom and I are giving out at presentation
- Plan how best to schedule assignment received today – deadline 3 weeks
- Download booklet from website ready for next Monday's class

Getting the most from work experience

On some BTEC First courses, all learners have to do a **work placement**. On others, they are recommended but not essential, or are required only for some optional units. If you are doing one, you need to prepare for it so that you get the most out of it. The checklists in this section will help.

BTEC FACT

If you need specific evidence from a work placement for a particular unit, your tutor may give you a logbook or work diary, and will tell you how you will be assessed in relation to the work that you will do.

Before you go checklist

1 Find out about the organisation by researching online.

2 Check that you have all the information you'll need about the placement.

3 Check the route you will need to take and how long it will take you. Always allow longer on the first day.

4 Check with your tutor what clothes are suitable and make sure you look the part.

5 Check that you know any rules or guidelines you must follow.

6 Check that you know what to do if you have a serious problem during the placement, such as being too ill to go to work.

7 Talk to your tutor if you have any special personal concerns.

8 Read the unit(s) that relate to your placement carefully. Highlight points you need to remember or refer to regularly.

9 Read the assessment criteria that relate to the unit(s) and use these to make a list of the information and evidence you'll need to obtain.

10 Your tutor will give you an official logbook or diary – or just use a notebook. Make notes each evening while things are fresh in your mind, and keep them safely.

While you're on work placement

Ideally, on your first day you'll be told about the business and what you'll be expected to do. You may even be allocated to one particular member of staff who will be your 'mentor'. However, not all firms operate like this and if everyone is very busy, your **induction** may be rushed. If so, stay positive and watch other people to see what they're doing. Then offer to help where you can.

TRY THIS

You're on work experience. The placement is interesting and related to the job you want to do. However, you've been watching people most of the time and want to get more involved. Identify three jobs you think you could offer to do.

While you're there

1. Arrive with a positive attitude, knowing that you are going to do your best and get the most out of your time there.
2. Although you may be nervous at first, don't let that stop you from smiling at people, saying 'hello' and telling them your name.
3. Arrive punctually – or even early – every day. If you're delayed for any reason, phone and explain. Then get there as soon as you can.
4. If you take your mobile phone, switch it off when you arrive.
5. If you have nothing to do, offer to help someone who is busy or ask if you can watch someone who is doing a job that interests you.
6. Always remember to thank people who give you information, show you something or agree that you can observe them.
7. If you're asked to do something and don't understand what to do, ask for it to be repeated. If it's complicated, write it down.
8. If a task is difficult, start it and then check back that you are doing it correctly before you go any further.
9. Obey all company rules, such as regulations and procedures relating to health and safety and using machinery, the use of IT equipment and access to confidential information.
10. Don't rush off as fast as you can at the end of the day. Check first with your mentor or supervisor whether you can leave.

Coping with problems

Problems are rare but can happen. The most common ones are being bored because you're not given any work to do or upset because you feel someone is treating you unfairly. Normally, the best first step is to talk to your mentor at work or your supervisor. However, if you're very worried or upset, you may prefer to get in touch with your tutor instead – do it promptly.

TOP TIP

Observing people who are skilled at what they do helps you learn a lot, and may even be part of your **assignment brief**.

Getting experience of work in the business sector

While studying for your BTEC First in Business, you may get the chance to go on work experience. If you are considering a particular career, this is an ideal way to see if you will actually enjoy the job. Even if your work experience is not in a job that you are seriously considering, you can still learn a great deal.

Activity: Are you prepared for work experience?

Answer the following questions to see how prepared you are for your work experience.

1 Decide if the statements **a–f** are **True** or **False**. Circle your chosen answer.

- **a)** While I am on work experience, I have to be on time every day. **True** **False**
- **b)** The routine will be completely different from school and my other day-to-day activities. **True** **False**
- **c)** It doesn't matter if I am disorganised. **True** **False**
- **d)** I will not have a chance to practise skills I learned in school or college. **True** **False**
- **e)** I will learn what employers expect from an employee and what I can expect from an employer. **True** **False**
- **f)** This opportunity will not automatically lead to a job. **True** **False**

2 Give two reasons why work experience can be of great benefit to you.

3 List three types of jobs that you would like to try during your work experience.

4 It's the day before you start your work experience. Which of these two statements comes closest to how you might be feeling? Put a tick next to your chosen statement.

- **a)** I'm a bit nervous but I'm really looking forward to starting my work experience. It will take me a while to get used to things but I'll soon make new friends and I'll learn new skills. I must look my best so that I make a good first impression. I'll be okay.
- **b)** I don't want to go on work experience. It will be boring. I'd rather stay home and watch the telly. They won't like me! They'll just boss me about and expect me to do stupid things.

5 It's your first morning on work experience and you have been asked to make tea for the boss and three colleagues. How would you deal with it? Put a tick next to your chosen statement.

a) Say 'get lost' and walk off in a huff.

b) Say 'make your own tea' and carry on with what you were doing.

c) Say 'of course' and spend the next half an hour wondering where the cups are, where the tea bags are, where the milk is, then burst into tears because you can't find the sugar.

d) Say 'yes, okay' but ask someone to show you where the things are and write down people's names with information about how they take their drink.

6 It is coming up to one o'clock on your first day and no one has mentioned your lunch break. Do you:

a) get up and walk out?

b) sit there feeling upset and hungry?

c) get out your packed lunch and start eating it?

d) ask someone else about lunchtimes and routines?

7 Given the choice of dealing with a positive, upbeat person with a 'can-do' attitude or dealing with a disgruntled, bored, uninterested person, which would you choose?

8 Most of us prefer to be around people with a positive attitude. Developing a good attitude can help you get more out of your work experience, and can benefit you in all areas of life:

- It makes you feel better.
- You can brighten other people's days.
- People want to be around those who have a good attitude.
- Employers want to employ people with a great attitude.
- Customers prefer to deal with positive people.

Use a highlighter pen to indicate which of these statements demonstrate an appropriate attitude to work experience.

a) Be enthusiastic and willing. Think about how your work will benefit others – this can help you to find job satisfaction even in menial tasks.

b) Just turn up and go through the motions until it is time to go home. Keep yourself to yourself.

c) Think about lessons learnt – even if something goes wrong or the placement isn't what you expected, you can still learn something from the experience.

d) Once something goes wrong, it's not worth continuing – you've blown it.

e) Listen carefully to what you're being told and ask if you don't understand something.

f) Just switch off and think about things you can do tonight with your friends.

g) Be friendly and smile! Smiling can actually make you happier.

h) Don't look too enthusiastic as colleagues may start taking advantage by asking you to do extra tasks.

9 The next activity examines how the skills you are learning at school or college and other aspects of your behaviour can be used effectively in your work experience. The table lists various skills and behaviours. Place a tick in the third column if you think the skill or behaviour would be useful while undertaking work experience.

	Skill or behaviour	Tick
A	Listening to what others have to say	
B	Arguing and shouting	
C	Speaking clearly	
D	Asking and responding to questions	
E	Keeping quiet, not contributing to work discussions	
F	Not answering the telephone if it rings	
G	Reading and responding to written material	
H	Using numbers	
I	Not recording or collecting data if asked	
J	Not presenting data as requested	
K	Not handling money carefully	
L	Refusing to operate a fax machine	

	Skill or behaviour	Tick
M	Pretending you do not know how to operate a computer	
N	Presenting information	
O	Taking responsibility if the team gives you a task	
P	Setting targets for yourself	
Q	Not cooperating with others in your team	
R	Not learning from others	
S	Not planning and managing your time	
T	Reviewing and evaluating your performance	
U	Not contributing to decision making	
V	Helping to solve problems	
W	Recognising problems	
X	Not looking for information	

Case study: Preparing for work experience

With the help of his tutor, Connor has arranged a placement within the marketing department of a large supermarket chain that has its head office near to his home. Connor has told the company that he would like to experience some of the activities that occur in the marketing department and his time has been planned accordingly. His work experience starts in four weeks' time.

He has been told that his work day will start at 9 am and that he must report to a junior manager in the department, who will look after him while on work experience. He can get a bus to his placement; one leaves a bus stop near his home at 8.40 am and will arrive at 9 am. There is an earlier bus that departs at 8.10 am. Which bus do you think Connor should catch? Why?

Connor feels very nervous about his placement as this is the first time that he has worked for a company and he really does not know what to expect. What could Connor do to find out more about the company before he starts his work experience? Think about what Connor should take with him on his first day.

Connor is hoping that he will be allowed to operate a computer as he feels he has good skills in this area. He would also like to know more about how retail prices are set as he has covered this topic within one of his BTEC First units. He is worried that people will not talk to him and he may be excluded from what is going on in the department. Connor's parents and tutor have assured him that staff will understand he is new and will go out of their way to make him feel at home.

BTEC FACT

An important part of your BTEC course is learning how to work positively and productively with other people.

Working with other people

Everyone finds it easy to work with people they like and far harder with those they don't. On your course you'll often be expected to work as a team to do a task. This gives you practice in working with different people.

You will be expected to:

- contribute to the task
- listen to other people's views
- adapt to other people's ways of working
- take responsibility for your own contribution
- agree the best way to resolve any problems.

These are quite complex skills. It helps if you understand the benefits to be gained by working cooperatively with other people and know the best way to achieve this.

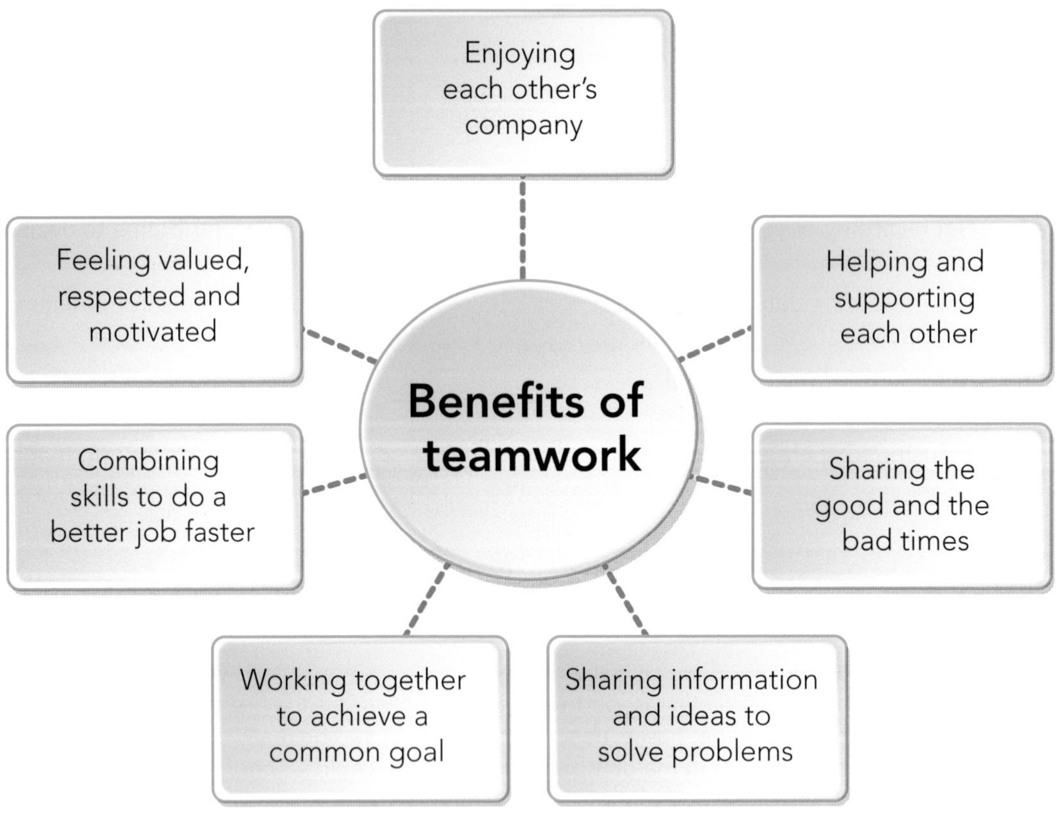

The benefits of good working relationships and teamwork.

Golden rules for everyone (including the team leader!)

The secret of a successful team is that everyone works together. The role of the team leader is to make this as easy as possible by listening to people's views and coordinating everyone's efforts. A team leader is not there to give orders.

Positive teamwork checklist

- ✔ Be loyal to your team, including the team leader.
- ✔ Be reliable and dependable at all times.
- ✔ Be polite. Remember to say 'please' and 'thank you'.
- ✔ Think before you speak.
- ✔ Treat everyone the same.
- ✔ Make allowances for individual personalities. Give people 'space' if they need it, but be ready to offer support if they ask for it.
- ✔ Admit mistakes and apologise if you've done something wrong – learn from it but don't dwell on it.
- ✔ Give praise when it's due, give help when you can and thank people who help you.
- ✔ Keep confidences, and any promises that you make.

TOP TIP

Being a good team member means putting the group's needs before your own.

TRY THIS

Work out whether you're usually passive, assertive or aggressive when you're annoyed. You've arranged to meet Sam to see a film. He arrives 20 minutes late.

Do you:

a) shrug and say nothing in case he gets upset

b) ask why he didn't text you to give you warning

c) say that it's the last time you'll ever go anywhere with him and walk off.

Which do you think would be the most effective – and why?

Case study: Teamworking in Business

Curtis, Maria, Fatima, Tom and Jake have formed a team to do some research. They have been asked to identify what types of businesses exist locally, their ownership and size. This is the first time the learners have had to work in a team and they are all a bit unsure about how to proceed. At their first meeting, Maria volunteers as team leader.

They begin by discussing what needs to be done. Tom suggests that they should all try to agree, as far as possible, when group decisions are made. Fatima emphasises that everyone's opinion should be taken into account and that it is important for group members to be punctual when meeting. They also decide that, in order for all members of the group to keep up-to-date, they will communicate regularly by email.

They decide on a clear objective: to visit 10 local businesses to find out about the size of each company and type of ownership.

Initially, they plan to identify 20 businesses from a local business directory and contact them by phone, giving 10 extra contacts just in case some businesses will not participate or are too busy to see them when they arrive.

Between them, they allocate the telephoning tasks. They also arrange a group meeting for the following day to draft a simple questionnaire to use in the interviews with the business representatives – they plan to divide up the interviews between the group members, but want to make sure that everyone asks the same questions.

One week later, they obtain their results and are able to complete their individual assignments.

There are many benefits to be gained from working as a team.

Activity: Effective and ineffective teams

The following activity contains a number of statements that describe effective and ineffective teams working in business. Place an 'E' next to a statement which describes an effective team and an 'I' next to the statements that describe ineffective teams.

1. The team consists of a range of individuals who contribute in different ways.
2. The overall output from the team is more than the sum of the individual contributions of members.
3. Clear goals are agreed – everyone understands and commits to them.
4. Some people talk more than they listen and only a few people are able to contribute.
5. Everyone understands the tasks they have to do and group members help each other.
6. Members don't assess how the group is working or talk about the problems it faces.
7. There is a supportive, informal atmosphere where members feel able to take risks and say what they think.
8. Different people assume the role of leader for different tasks.
9. Members' ideas are dismissed or even ridiculed, and their views are ignored.
10. Some members are silent and don't contribute.
11. The group is comfortable with disagreement and can successfully overcome differences in opinion.
12. There is a lot of discussion in which everyone participates.
13. Group members listen to each other and everyone's ideas are heard.
14. There are arguments between members of the group.
15. Disagreements are put to the vote without being discussed.
16. There is a lack of trust and helpfulness.
17. Roles are not delegated to particular team members.
18. One or two members dominate the others and make the decisions.
19. Members feel free to criticise and say what they think, but this is done in a positive, constructive manner.
20. Some members are unhappy with decisions and grumble privately afterwards.
21. Little effort is made to keep discussions to the point or to work to deadlines.
22. The group learns from experience, reviewing and improving performance in the light of both successes and failures.
23. There is a lack of clarity regarding goals and specific tasks are not agreed.

Getting the most from special events

BTEC First courses usually include several practical activities and special events. These enable you to find out information, develop your skills and knowledge in new situations and enjoy new experiences. They may include visits to external venues, visits from specialist speakers, and team events.

Industry visits give you the opportunity to see first hand how businesses operate.

Most learners enjoy the chance to do something different. You'll probably look forward to some events more than others. If you're ready to get actively involved, you'll usually gain the most benefit. It also helps to make a few preparations!

Case study: Visiting a manufacturing plant

A BTEC First tutor has arranged for the class to visit a medium-sized food-manufacturing plant. Learners will have an opportunity to collect evidence for an assignment dealing with people's roles in organisations. The human resource manager is going to give the class a tour of the plant and will then give a presentation on the different roles and responsibilities of the staff.

Before the visit, the tutor holds a class discussion to agree the rules for the trip. In this way, the group takes ownership of the rules and agrees that they will apply to everyone.

The class think being punctual for the bus that will take them to the plant is a must. They also agree that, although one or two members of the class have doubts about whether the trip will be worthwhile, they will all go with open minds. The tutor reminds them that they should take a notepad and pen, and that the aim is to find out about the various roles and responsibilities that people perform in the business. The class agree to prepare questions in advance, which they will do in small groups. One member of the class volunteers to thank the human resource manager for the tour and presentation.

After the visit, the tutor holds a group discussion, and hears that everyone found the experience very enjoyable. The class learned a lot about the different roles and responsibilities that are in place within the business.

One of the learners who originally had doubts about the visit comments:

'I think I got this one wrong, I thought I could get just as much information from the internet. The visit has really opened my eyes about how a manufacturing organisation is organised and the vast range of roles and responsibilities that exist. My assignment will be much easier to put together now.'

Special events checklist

- ✔ Check you understand how the event relates to your course.
- ✔ If a visit or trip is not something you would normally find very interesting, try to keep an open mind. You might get a surprise!
- ✔ Find out what you're expected to do, and any rules or guidelines you must follow, including about your clothes or appearance.
- ✔ Always allow enough time to arrive five minutes early, and make sure you're never late.
- ✔ On an external visit, make notes on what you see and hear. This is essential if you have to write about it afterwards, use your information to answer questions in an assignment or do something practical.
- ✔ If an external speaker is going to talk to your class, prepare a list of questions in advance. Nominate someone to thank the speaker afterwards. If you want to record the talk, it's polite to ask first.
- ✔ For a team event, you may be involved in planning and helping to allocate different team roles. You'll be expected to participate positively in any discussions, to talk for some (but not all) of the time, and perhaps to volunteer for some jobs yourself.
- ✔ Write up any notes you make as soon as you can – while you can still understand what you wrote!

At the last minute, you're asked to propose a vote of thanks to a visiting speaker on behalf of your class. What would you say?

Activity: Preparing for excursions and visiting speakers

You have to complete an assignment that involves finding about the different ways in which businesses can be owned and classified. Your tutor invites a self-employed management consultant to come in and deliver a presentation on this topic. Your tutor also arranges for your class to visit three local businesses, which are owned in different ways and fall within different classifications.

These statements are about preparing for visiting speakers and excursions. Please consider whether each statement is **True** or **False**. Circle your chosen answer.

1. These excursions and talks from outside speakers do not give any information and do not allow you to develop your skills. **True** **False**
2. You should always prepare for these events by thinking about questions you could ask and identifying in advance the information you need to find out. **True** **False**
3. Visiting speakers and excursions play no part in the preparation for my assignments. **True** **False**
4. You should listen carefully to everything that is said or discussed. **True** **False**
5. You should always be punctual for outside visits. **True** **False**
6. You must always behave impeccably when a speaker comes in and when you visit businesses. **True** **False**
7. It is not worth taking a pen or notepad on visits or to talks by visiting speakers. **True** **False**
8. You should write up notes carefully and as soon as possible after the event. **True** **False**
9. You don't have to take notes as you can always email the visiting speaker to get information. **True** **False**
10. You should ask questions about anything you do not understand. **True** **False**

Resources and research

Understanding resources

Resources are items that help you do something. The most obvious one is money! To obtain your BTEC First award, however, your resources are rather different.

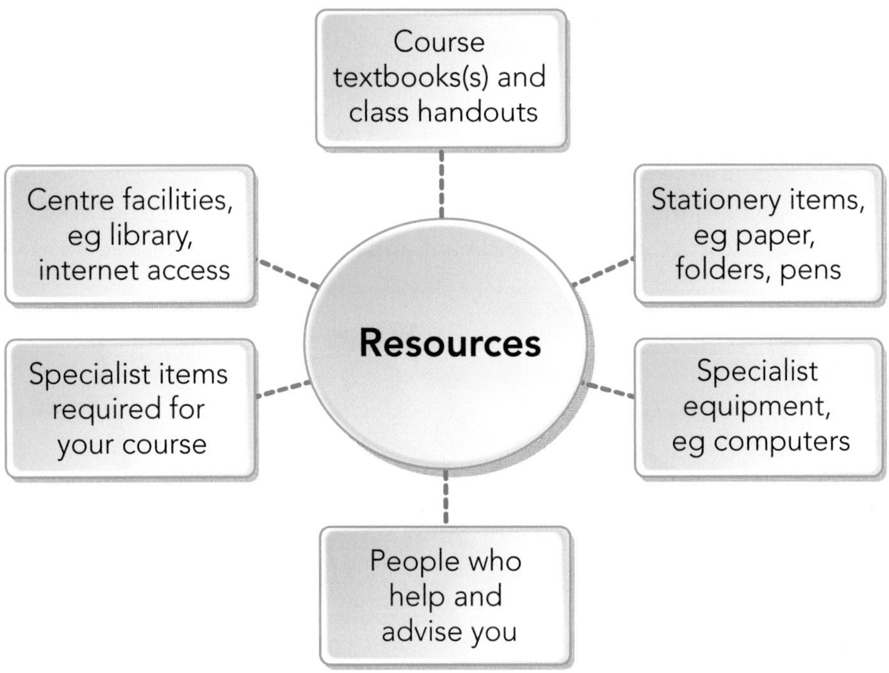

Different kinds of resources

Physical resources

Physical resources are things like textbooks, computers and any specialist equipment.

- Popular textbooks, laptops for home use and specialist equipment may need to be booked. Leaving it until the last minute is risky.
- You can ask for help if you don't know how to use resources properly.
- You should check what stationery and equipment you need at the start of your course and make sure you have it.
- You need to look after your resources carefully. This saves money and time spent replacing lost items.

TOP TIP

Life is a lot easier if you have all the resources you need and you take care of them. Lending important notes can hold you up (so photocopy them instead). Lending your course book may mean you can't complete work you have to do. Lending one of your assignments could get you in serious trouble!

People as resources

There are many people who can help you through your course:

- family members who help and support you
- your tutor
- friends in your group who collect handouts for you and phone you to keep you up to date when you're absent
- librarians and computer technicians, at your centre or your local library
- expert practitioners.

Expert practitioners

Expert practitioners have worked hard to be successful in their chosen area. They know the skills and knowledge needed to do the job properly. They can be invaluable when you're researching information. You can also learn a lot by watching them at work, especially if you can ask them questions about what they do, what they find hard and any difficulties they've had.

A marketing executive must have the confidence and expertise to give presentations to large or small groups of colleagues.

Try to observe more than one expert practitioner:

- It gives you a better picture about what they do.
- No single job will cover all aspects of work that might apply to your studies.
- You may find some experts more approachable and easy to understand than others. For example, if someone is impatient because they're busy it may be difficult to ask them questions, or if someone works very quickly you may find it hard to follow what they're doing.

If you have problems, just note what you've learnt and compare it with your other observations. And there's always the chance that you're observing someone who's not very good at their job! You'll only know this for certain if you've seen what people should be doing.

TRY THIS

You may not have to make a special visit to observe an expert practitioner at work. Often television programmes (and YouTube clips) give great insights into the way a job can or should be done. See if you can find clips of someone you admire in your own vocational area by putting their name into the search facility in YouTube or Google.

Activity: Create your own resource list

You have been asked by your tutor to investigate any large multinational company and you have selected Tesco plc. You have been asked to gather the following information:

1 the size of the business in terms of financial turnover, number of employees and the number of countries in which it operates
2 the attitude of the staff to working for the company
3 the types of products made or sold, or services provided.

A visiting speaker will be coming to talk about Tesco plc and the manager of the local store has given you permission to interview some of the staff. Part of the activity will include giving a presentation to the rest of the class on the information you have gathered.

Resources for your BTEC First course overall and for completing this assignment in particular will vary enormously. Resources could include the handouts you are given by your tutor, the equipment and facilities at your school or college, information from the internet or from people you interview, and books, magazines and journals.

This activity will guide you through the first step in preparing for the assignment outlined above – drawing up a resource list. You must identify all the possible resources that you will need to access. Do not include general resources such as pen, paper and computers; concentrate on resources that are directly related to this assignment.

1 Identify two websites that will give you information about Tesco plc and, for each website, briefly describe what information is given.
   a) Website 1

   b) Website 2

2 Identify two books from the library that contain relevant information about Tesco plc and, for each book, describe the information given.
   a) Book 1

b) Book 2

3 Identify two newspaper or journal articles that contain information on Tesco plc and, for each article, describe the information given.

a) Journal/Newspaper 1

b) Journal/Newspaper 2

4i) List three questions you would ask the visiting speaker to help you complete your activity.

a)

b)

c)

ii) List three relevant questions you would ask Tesco's staff.

a)

b)

c)

5 Describe two resources you would use to give your presentation.

a) Resource 1

b) Resource 2

When completing your own assignments, you would check with your tutor to make sure that sources of information you have identified on your resource list are relevant to the assignment you have been set.

Finding the information you need

The information explosion

There are lots of different ways to find out information – books, newspapers, magazines, TV, radio, CDs, DVDs, the internet. And you can exchange information with other people by texting, sending an email or phoning someone.

All this makes it much easier to obtain information. If you know what you're doing, you can probably find most of what you need sitting at a computer. But there are some dangers:

- Finding exactly what you want online takes skill. You need to know what you're doing.
- It's easy to get too much information and become overwhelmed.
- It's unlikely that everything you need will be available online.
- The information you read may be out of date.
- The information may be neither reliable nor true.

Define what you are trying to find. (The more precise you are, the more likely you are to find what you're looking for.)

Know where to look for it. (Remember: the internet is not the only source of information.)

Recognise when you have found appropriate information.

Know what to do with information once you've found it. (Make sure that you understand it, interpret it correctly and record the source where you found it.)

Know when to stop looking (especially if you have a deadline).

Before you start

There are four things that will help you look in the right place and target your search properly.

Ask yourself ...	Because ...	Example
Exactly what do I need to find out?	It will save you time and effort.	If you need information about accidents, you need to know what type of accident and over what time period.
Why do I need this information and who is going to read it?	This puts the task into context. You need to identify the best type of information to obtain and how to get it.	If you're making a poster or leaflet for children, you'll need simple information that can be presented in a graphical format. If, however, you're giving a workplace presentation on accidents, you'll need tables and graphs to illustrate your talk.
Where can I find it?	You need to consider whether your source is trustworthy and up to date. The internet is great, but you must check that the sites you use are reliable.	To find out about accidents in the workplace you could talk to the health and safety at work officer. To find examples of accidents in your local area you could look through back copies of your local newspaper in the local library or newspaper offices.
What is my deadline?	You know how long you have to find the information and use it.	

TRY THIS

Schedule your research time by calculating backwards from the deadline date. Split the time you have 50/50 between searching for information and using it. This stops you searching for too long and getting lots of interesting material, but then not having the time to use it properly!

Your three main sources of information are:

- libraries or learning resource centres
- the internet
- asking other people, for example through interviews and questionnaires.

Researching in libraries

You can use the learning resource centre in your school or college, or a local public library. Public libraries usually have a large reference section with many resources available for loan, including CD-ROMs, encyclopaedias, government statistics, magazines, journals and newspapers, and databases such as Infotrac, which contains articles from newspapers and magazines over the last five years.

The librarian will show you how to find the resources you need and how to look up a specific book (or author) to check if it is available or is out on loan.

Some books and resources can only be used in the library itself, while others can be taken out on short-term or long-term loan. You need to plan how to access and use the resources that are popular or restricted.

Using your library

- ✔ If your centre has an intranet you might be able to check which books and CD-ROMs are available without actually visiting the library.
- ✔ All libraries have photocopying facilities, so take enough change with you to copy articles that you can't remove. Write down the source of any article you photocopy, ie the name and the date of the publication.
- ✔ Learn how to keep a reference file (or bibliography) in which you store the details of all your sources and references. A bibliography must include CDs, DVDs and other information formats, not just books and magazines.
- ✔ If your search is complicated, go at a quiet time when the librarian can help you.
- ✔ Don't get carried away if you find several books that contain the information you need. Too many can be confusing.
- ✔ Use the index to find information quickly by searching for key words. Scan the index using several likely alternatives.
- ✔ Only use books that you find easy to understand. A book is only helpful if you can retell the information in your own words.

Researching online

A good search engine such as Google will help you find useful websites. They look for sites based on the information you enter in the search box. In some cases, such as Ask.co.uk, you may get the chance to refine your choice after entering your key words or question.

Finding information on a website

Wikipedia is a popular free online encyclopaedia. It has been criticised because entries may be inaccurate as members of the public can edit the site. However, Wikipedia is trying to prevent this by organising professional editing.

If you're not sure whether something you read is correct, or if there is anything strange about it, check it against information on another site. Make sure you ask your tutor's opinion, too.

With large websites, it can be difficult to find what you need. Always read the whole screen – there may be several menus in different parts of the screen.

To help you search, many large websites have:

- their own search facility or a site map that lists site content with links to the different pages
- links to similar sites where you might find more information. Clicking a link should open a new window, so you'll still be connected to the original site.

TRY THIS

Search engines don't just find websites. On Google, the options at the top of your screen include 'images', 'news' and 'maps'. If you click on 'more' and then 'even more', you'll find other options, too. You'll usually find the most relevant information if you use the UK version of a search engine. Only search the whole web if you deliberately want to include European and American information. To see this in action, go to www.pearsonhotlinks.co.uk, insert the express code 5780S and click on the link for this page.

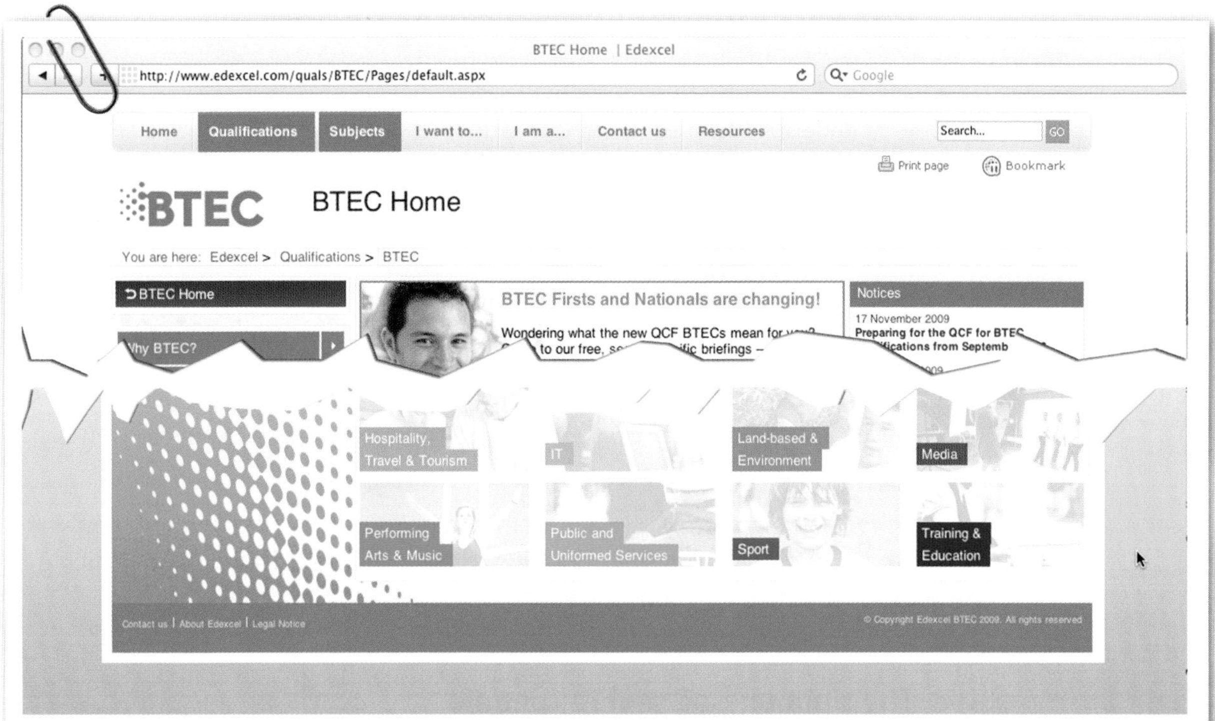

There may be useful information at the foot and either side of a web page.

There are several other useful sites you can visit when researching online.

- **Directory sites** show websites in specific categories so you can focus your search at the start.
- **Forums** are sites, or areas of a website, where people post comments on an issue. They can be useful if you want to find out opinions on a topic. You can usually read them without registering.
- **News sites** include the BBC website as well as the sites for all the daily newspapers. Check the website of your local newspaper, too.

Printing information

- Only print information that you're sure will be useful. It's easy to print too much and find yourself drowning in paper.
- Make quick notes on your print-outs so that you remember why you wanted them. It will jog your memory when you're sorting through them later.
- If there's a printer-friendly option, use it. It will give you a print-out without unnecessary graphics or adverts.
- Check the bottom line of your print-outs. It should show the URL for that page of the website, and the date. You need those if you have to list your sources or if you want to quote from the page.

TRY THIS

To see how directory sites work go to www.pearsonhotlinks.co.uk, insert the express code 5780S and click on the link for this page.

TOP TIP

Bookmark sites you use regularly by adding the URL to your browser. How to do this will depend on which browser you use, eg Internet Explorer, Firefox.

Researching by asking other people

You're likely to do this for two reasons:

- you need help from someone who knows a lot about a topic.
- you need to find out several people's opinions on something.

Information from an expert

Explain politely why you are carrying out the investigation. Ask questions slowly and clearly about what they do and how they do it. If they don't mind, you could take written notes so you remember what they tell you. Put the name and title of the person, and the date, at the top. This is especially important if you might be seeing more than one person, to avoid getting your notes muddled up.

Ask whether you may contact them again, in case there's anything you need to check. Write down their phone number or email address. Above all, remember to say 'thank you'!

The opinions of several people

The easiest way to do this is with a questionnaire. You can either give people the questionnaire to complete themselves or interview them and complete it yourself. Professional interviewers often telephone people to ask questions, but at this stage it's not a good idea unless you know the people you're phoning and they're happy for you to do this.

TOP TIP

Design your questionnaire so that you get quantifiable answers. This means you can easily add them up to get your final result.

TRY THIS

Always test your draft questionnaire on several people, to highlight any confusing questions or instructions.

Devising a questionnaire

1. Make sure it has a title and clear instructions.
2. Rather than ask for opinions, give people options, eg yes/no, maybe/always, never/sometimes. This will make it easier to analyse the results.
3. Or you can ask interviewees to give a score, say out of 5, making it clear what each number represents, eg 5 = excellent, 3 = very good.
4. Keep your questionnaire short so that your interviewees don't lose interest. Between 10 and 15 questions is probably about right, as long as that's enough to find out all you need.
5. Remember to add 'thank you' at the end.
6. Decide upon the representative sample of people you will approach. These are the people whose views are the most relevant to the topic you're investigating.
7. Decide how many responses you need to get a valid answer. This means that the answer is representative of the wider population. For example, if you want views on food in your canteen, it's pointless only asking five people. You might pick the only five people who detest (or love) the food it serves.

Case study: Designing and testing questionnaires

Imran is studying for a BTEC First in Business at his local comprehensive school. As part of one of his assignments looking at good customer care, he is carrying out some research. This involves producing a questionnaire to interview shoppers outside a local supermarket. He also wants to ask the customer services manager about the customer care training the business provides for its staff. The first thing that Imran has to do is contact the store manager to explain his project and ask for permission to carry out the interviews.

Imran then designs two questionnaires: one to interview the customers and one for the customer services manager. The two questionnaires have different questions and the form for the customer services manager has spaces for the name and job title of the person he will be interviewing. He decides to use multiple-choice answers on the questionnaire for the customers, to make it easier to analyse. If you were Imran, how would you test your questionnaire before using it on customers? Think about the questions Imran might ask the customers. How will these differ from his questions to the customer services manager?

Activity: Research

The following activity illustrates the importance of research when completing a BTEC First in Business.

Sony Music Entertainment UK is part of one of the largest music and entertainment organisations in the world. Your tutor has asked you to find out more about this company. In particular you have to find out about:

1 the size of Sony Music Entertainment UK and some information about the organisation that owns the company
2 the kind of things the company does
3 three recording artists that you like who are signed by this company.

Get on the internet, find the company website of Sony Music Entertainment UK and have a go at tasks 1–3. Note down your answers in the spaces provided below.

1

2

3

Think of five questions to ask other learners in your centre to find out how much they know about Sony Music Entertainment UK, and whether they are aware that the artists you have identified are signed by this company.

1

2

3

4

5

Interview ten learners and summarise your results below.

Workshops

During your BTEC First you will have the opportunity to attend workshops. A workshop is a short series of educational and work sessions. Small groups of learners meet together to concentrate on a defined area of concern, such as problem solving or planning a project. Workshops may also be used for coverage of functional skills, including ICT.

Keeping a logbook

You may be asked to complete a logbook as part of the BTEC First programme. You could use a notebook or loose leaves in a ring binder to make daily entries of your learning experiences. By regularly reading through your notes, you can monitor your progress throughout the course. Used like a diary, the logbook is an excellent way of keeping track of your experiences and feelings about how the course is progressing.

Managing your information

Whether you've found lots of information or only a little, assessing what you have and using it wisely is very important. This section will help you avoid the main pitfalls.

Organising and selecting your information

Organising your information

The first step is to organise your information so that it's easy to use.

- Make sure your written notes are neat and have a clear heading – it's often useful to date them, too.
- Note useful pages in any books or magazines you have borrowed.
- Highlight relevant parts of any handouts or leaflets.
- Work out the results of any questionnaires you've used.

Manual and electronic organisation

For your BTEC First in Business you will need to learn how to organise and file your information, both manually and electronically. During the course, you will produce – and want to save – a significant amount of information which may be useful for assignments.

It is important, right from the outset, that you start filing electronic information effectively:

- Save important website addresses, electronic documents such as draft assignments, and other information that you have gathered electronically.
- For easy access, it is advisable to save the information in electronic folders named after the unit numbers and titles.

Similarly, you will have lots of paper-based information to organise. Effective file management is just as important for non-electronic information:

- Always have your files well organised.
- Use unit numbers to divide up your file.
- Always store your handouts and notes in the correct section, so you can refer to them at a later date.
- Try to find somewhere at home where you can safely file larger documents, such as journal or newspaper articles.

Selecting your information

Re-read the **assignment brief** or instructions you were given to remind yourself of the exact wording of the question(s) and divide your information into three groups:

1 Information that is totally relevant.
2 Information that is not as good, but could come in useful.
3 Information that doesn't match the questions or assignment brief very much but that you kept because you couldn't find anything better!

Check there are no obvious gaps in your information against the questions or assignment brief. If there are, make a note of them so that you know exactly what you still have to find. Although it's ideal to have everything you need before you start work, don't delay if you're short of time.

Putting your information in order

Putting your information in a logical order means you can find what you want easily. It will save you time in the long run. This is doubly important if you have lots of information and will be doing the work over several sessions.

Case study: Getting organised

Before joining the BTEC First in Business, Harry was very disorganised; his loose notes were just crammed into his bag and he never filed anything, even though his parents had bought him a number of ring binders.

When the time came for Harry to start work on his first assignment, he began to panic as he could not find any of his notes or handouts. His electronic organisation was no better – he couldn't remember where on the computer he had saved important pieces of information for the assignment. Harry went to see his tutor about the problem.

'I sat down with the tutor, who reminded me of what we had learnt in the induction programme about being organised and how "failing to plan was planning to fail". He advised me to be more organised with my notes and handouts, and to plan my work using timelines to help me complete projects on time.

Similarly, with stored information on the computer, I was told to save documents into clearly identified files so that I would be able to retrieve the information easily. It took a lot of practice to change my habits but, with perseverance, I am now far more organised. I have even started to tidy up my bedroom regularly so I don't go into a blind panic when I want to find something!'

Activity: Relative importance

Try this exercise dealing with the organisation of information according to its relative importance.

You are researching how the charity Oxfam manages its business. You have found six pieces of information:

1. 30 pages from an online news agency about how, since the start of the Credit Crunch in 2007, Oxfam has received less money from donations
2. an article discussing why one of the charity's volunteers is getting an award
3. a five-page article produced by Oxfam which discusses how the business is managed internationally
4. a handout from the manager of the local branch who came to talk to the group about Oxfam and how it is run
5. a handout from the tutor describing charities generally, but not referring directly to Oxfam
6. an article you found in the national press announcing that Oxfam in London is moving to a new site.

Write a couple of sentences describing how useful each of the six pieces of information is for the research task.

1

2

3

4

5

6

Hopefully, you will have identified that some of the documents are more helpful for this task than others. It is, however, worth noting that all information, no matter how irrelevant it may seem when you find it, could contain something that might be useful for a future assignment. So, file it where you will be able to find it!

Interpreting and presenting your information

The next stage is to use your information to prepare the document and/or oral presentation you have to give. There are four steps:

1 Understand what you're reading.

2 Interpret what you're reading.

3 Know the best form in which to produce the information, bearing in mind the purpose for which it is required.

4 Create the required document so that it's in a suitable layout with correct spelling and punctuation.

Understanding what you read

As a general rule, never use information that you don't understand. However, nobody understands complex or unfamiliar material the first time they read it, especially if they just scan through it quickly. Before you reject it, try this:

Read it once to get the main idea.

Read it again, slowly, to try to take in more detail.

Look up any words you don't know in a dictionary to find out what they mean.

Read it a third time and underline or highlight the main points. (If this is a book or magazine that you shouldn't write in, take a photocopy first and write on that.)

Summarise the main points in your own words.

Write your own version.

Special note: Show both the article and your own version to your tutor to check your understanding. This will help you identify any points you missed out and help you improve your skills of interpreting and summarising.

Understanding unfamiliar information

Interpreting what you read

Interpreting what you read is different from understanding it. This is because you can't always take it for granted that something you read means what it says. The writer may have had a very strong or biased opinion, or may have exaggerated for effect. This doesn't mean that you can't use the information.

BTEC FACT

In your assignments, it's better to separate opinions from facts. If you're quoting someone's views, make this clear.

Strong opinions and bias

People often have strong points of view about certain topics. This may be based on reliable facts, but not always! We can all jump to conclusions that may not be very logical, especially if we feel strongly about something.

Things aren't always what they seem to be. Are these boys fighting or are they having a good time?

TRY THIS

There are many scare stories in the media about issues such as immigration, children's reading ability or obesity. Next time you're watching television and these are discussed, see if you can spot biased views, exaggeration and claims without any supporting evidence.

Exaggeration

Many newspapers exaggerate facts to startle and attract their readers.

LOCAL FIRM DOUBLES STAFF IN TWO WEEKS!

This newspaper headline sounds very positive. You could easily think it means employment is growing and there are more jobs in your area. Then you read on, and find the firm had only four staff and now has eight!

TOP TIP

Never make assumptions or jump to conclusions. Make sure you have all the evidence to support your views.

Tables and graphs

You need to be able to interpret what the figures mean, especially when you look at differences between columns or rows. For example, your friend might have an impressive spreadsheet that lists his income and expenditure. In reality, it doesn't tell you much until you add the figures up and subtract one from the other. Only then can you say whether he is getting into debt. And even if he is, you need to see his budget over a few months, rather than just one which may be exceptional.

Choosing a format

You may have been given specific instructions about the format and layout of a document you have to produce, in which case life is easy as long as you follow them! If not, think carefully about the best way to set out your information so that it is clear.

Different formats	Example
text	when you write in paragraphs or prepare a report or summary
graphical	a diagram, graph or chart
pictorial	a drawing, photograph, cartoon or pictogram
tabular	numerical information in a table

The best method(s) will depend on the information you have, the source(s) of your material and the purpose of the document – a leaflet for schoolchildren needs graphics and pictures to make it lively, whereas a report to company shareholders would be mainly in text form with just one or two graphs.

Stating your sources

Whatever format you use, if you are including other people's views, comments or opinions, or copying a table or diagram from another publication, you must state the source by including the name of the author, publication or the web address. This can be in the text or as part of a list at the end. Failure to do this (so you are really pretending other people's work is your own) is known as **plagiarism**. It is a serious offence with penalties to match.

TOP TIP

Don't just rely on your spellchecker. It won't find a word spelled wrongly that makes another valid word (eg from/form), so you must proofread everything. And remember to check whether it is set to check American English or British English. There are some spelling differences.

Text format

Creating written documents gets easier with practice. These points should help.

Golden rules for written documents

1. Think about who will be reading it, then write in an appropriate language and style.
2. Ensure it is technically correct, ie no wrong spellings or bad punctuation.
3. Take time to make it look good, with clear headings, consistent spacing and plenty of white space.
4. Write in paragraphs, each with a different theme. Leave a line space between each one.
5. If you have a lot of separate points to mention, use bullets or numbered points. Numbered points show a certain order or quantity (step 1, step 2, etc). Use bullet points when there is no suggested order.
6. Only use words that you understand the meaning of, or it might look as if you don't know what you mean.
7. Structure your document so that it has a beginning, middle and end.
8. Prepare a draft and ask your tutor to confirm you are on the right track and are using your information in the best way.

Graphical format

TRY THIS

Someone asks for directions to your house. Would you write a list or draw a diagram? Which would be easier for you and for the other person – and why?

Most people find graphics better than a long description for creating a quick picture in the viewer's mind. There are several types of graphical format, and you can easily produce any of these if you have good ICT skills.

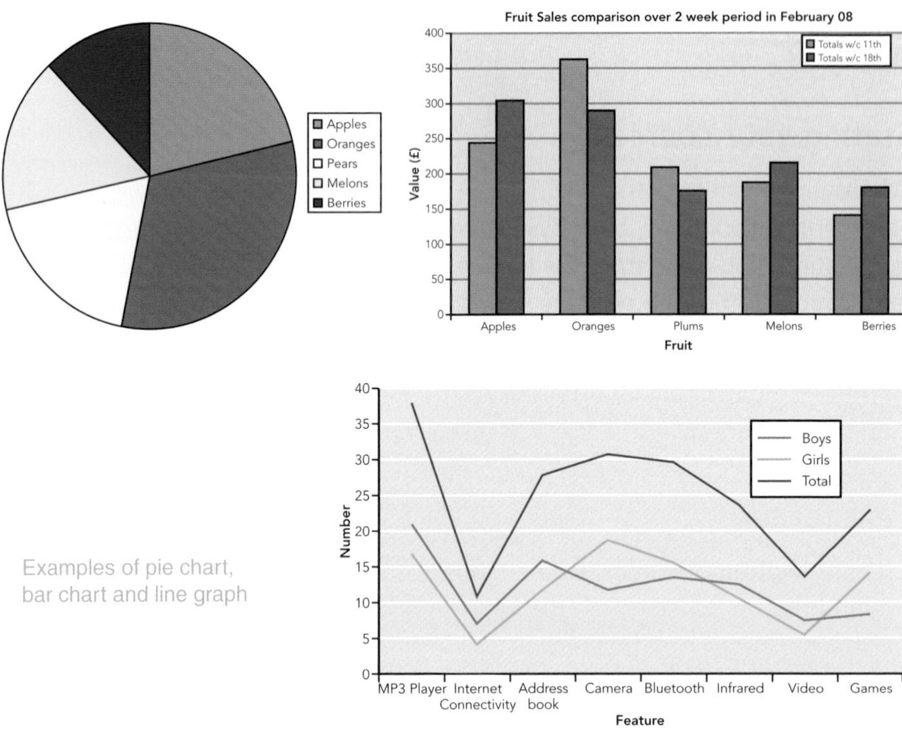

Examples of pie chart, bar chart and line graph

Pictorial format

Newspapers and magazines use pictures to illustrate situations and reduce the amount of words needed. It doesn't always have to be photographs though. For example, a new building may be sketched to show what it will look like.

A pictogram or pictograph is another type of pictorial format, such as charts which use the image of an object (fruit, coins, even pizzas) to represent data, such as the number eaten or amount spent.

TOP TIP

Don't spend hours writing text when an illustration can do the job better – but make sure the illustration you choose is suitable for the document and the reader.

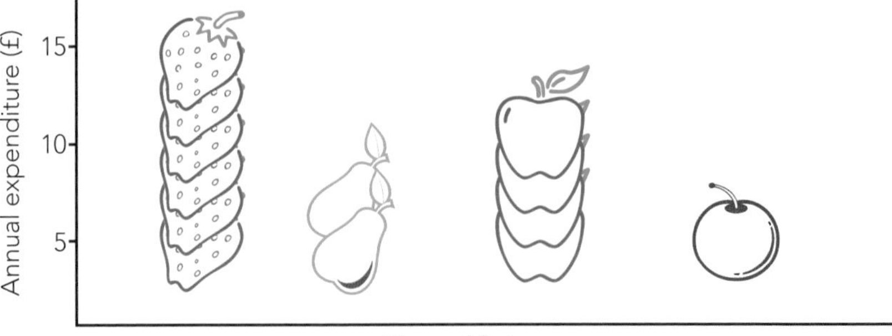

Tabular format

A table can be an easy way to communicate information. Imagine a retailer preparing information about the items in stock. Text would be difficult to understand and comparisons between stock levels and sales would be almost impossible to make. A table, however, would easily show the fastest-selling items.

Tables are also ideal if you are showing rankings – such as best-selling music or books.

Bestsellers list – September 2009

Position	Title	Author	Imprint	Publication
1 (New)	Lost Symbol,The	Brown, Dan	Bantam Press	15-Sep-2009
2 (1)	Complaints, The	Rankin, Ian	Orion	03-Sep-2009
3 (New)	Return Journey, The	Binchy, Maeve	Orion	17-Sep-2009
4 (7)	Sapphire	Price, Katie	Century	30-Jul-2009
5 (9)	Wolf Hall	Mantel, Hilary	Fourth Estate	30-Apr-2009
6 (3)	Week in December, A	Faulks, Sebastian	Hutchinson	03-Sep-2009
7 (2)	Alex Cross's Trial	Patterson, James	Century	10-Sep-2009
8 (4)	White Queen, The	Gregory, Philippa	Simon & Schuster Ltd	18-Aug-2009
9 (5)	Even Money	Francis, Dick & Francis, Felix	Michael Joseph	03-Sep-2009
10 (8)	206 Bones	Reichs, Kathy	William Heinemann	27-Aug-2009

National newspaper circulation – September 2009

	August 2009	August 2008	% change on last year	August 09 (without bulks)	March 2009 – August 2009	% change on last year
Sun	3,128,501	3,148,792	-0.64	3,128,501	3,052,480	-2.25
Daily Mail	2,171,686	2,258,843	-3.86	2,044,079	2,178,462	-4.45
Daily Mirror	1,324,883	1,455,270	-8.96	1,324,883	1,331,108	9.44
Daily Star	886,814	751,494	18.01	886,814	855,511	16.65
The Daily Telegraph	814,087	860,298	-5.37	722,644	807,328	-6.73
Daily Express	730,234	748,664	-2.46	730,234	727,824	-1.32
Times	576,185	612,779	-5.97	529,746	588,471	-4.63
Financial Times	395,845	417,570	-5.2	365,269	411,098	-6.7
Daily Record	347,302	390,197	-10.99	345,277	350,306	-10.59
Guardian	311,387	332,587	-6.37	311,387	332,790	-4.11
Independent	187,837	230,033	-18.34	148,551	198,445	-16.76

Activity: Interpreting information

1 The following is a quote from the sales director of a large washing-powder manufacturer about a new product that the company has just launched.

'BRILYANT is a fantastic new soap powder launched last month by our company. Our research shows that it the best stain remover and general purpose washing powder on the market. It is lower priced than its competitors and, in every one of our tests, it has beaten its competitors for whiteness, softness and value for money.'

a) As an exercise in understanding what the sales director is trying to say, summarise in your own words what you think she means.

b) Why do you have to be careful when using this type of information in an assignment?

c) Why do you think the sales director might exaggerate the qualities of the new product?

2 Lucy has obtained the following information about the sales of soft drinks from her local supermarket in the last week.

Day of week	Bottles sold
Monday	100
Tuesday	120
Wednesday	120
Thursday	250
Friday	300
Saturday	350
Sunday	120

a) During the BTEC First, you will often be asked to turn information into a graph or bar chart. Use Lucy's information to plot a simple bar chart in the space below.

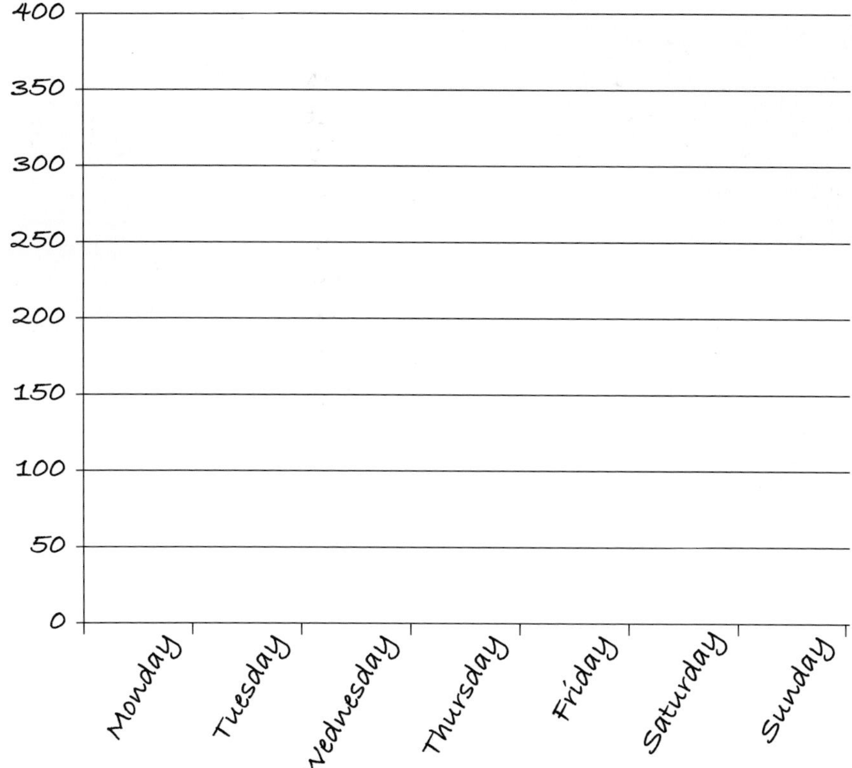

b) Which day has the best sales of soft drinks?

c) Which day has the worst sales of soft drinks?

d) Lucy knew that Thursday, Friday and Saturday were very hot summer days. How could this factor affect sales on these days?

4 According to the aim of a task and the data you are handling, you will need to use a variety of different methods to display your information in the most effective fashion.

For each of the examples below, indicate the most appropriate format. Use the following shorthand: Tx (text), G (graphical), P (pictorial) and Tab (tabular). If there is more than one possibility, you can give more than one answer.

a) a formal report for part of an assignment

b) financial information over a five-year period

c) a poster with artwork

d) a summary of an article for an assignment

e) monthly sales figures over 12 months for a local supermarket

f) a flow chart showing how a business is structured.

Making presentations

Presentations help you to learn communication skills.

Some people hate the idea of standing up to speak in front of an audience. This is quite normal, and you can use the extra energy from nerves to improve your performance.

Presentations aren't some form of torture devised by your tutor! They are included in your course because they help you learn many skills, such as speaking in public and preparing visual aids. They also help you practise working as a team member and give you a practical reason for researching information. And it can be far more enjoyable to talk about what you've found out rather than write about it!

There's a knack to preparing and giving a presentation so that you use your energies well, don't waste time, don't fall out with everyone around you and keep your stress levels as low as possible. Think about the task in three stages: preparation, organisation and delivery.

Preparation

Start your initial preparations as soon as you can. Putting them off will only cause problems later. Discuss the task in your team so that everyone is clear about what has to be done and how long you have to do it in.

Divide any research fairly among the team, allowing for people's strengths and weaknesses. You'll also need to agree:

- which visual aids would be best
- which handouts you need and who should prepare them
- where and when the presentation will be held, and what you should wear
- what questions you might be asked, both individually and as a team, and how you should prepare for them.

Once you've decided all this, carry out the tasks you've been allocated to the best of your ability and by the deadline agreed.

TOP TIP

Keep visual aids simple but effective and check any handouts carefully before you make lots of copies.

Organisation

This is about the planning you need to do as a team so that everything will run smoothly on the day.

Delivery

This refers to your performance during the presentation. Being well prepared and well organised helps stop you panicking. If you're very nervous at the start, take a few deep breaths and concentrate on the task, not yourself. It's quite normal to be nervous at the start but this usually fades once you get under way. You might even enjoy it …

Case study: Giving a presentation

As part of an assignment, Lara has to give a presentation on the purposes of business. The presentation is a team exercise and all members of the group will participate in all aspects of the task.

Although Lara is quite nervous, she has been reassured by her tutor, who told her that everyone feels the same and that her classmates understand presentations can be a bit of an ordeal for some people.

Lara's team mates decides to plan well in advance and have remembered what their tutor has said about being prepared and organised, which will help them to give a better delivery of the presentation. Lara outlines what they have done so far:

'We have divided the research work fairly among the team and allowed members of the group to select tasks which are suited to their strengths. We have agreed the method of presentation, which is PowerPoint. Two members of the team are responsible for preparing handouts and the others are drawing up a list of possible questions that we may be asked.

We have decided to use prompt cards and I was given the task of writing them out as my handwriting is the neatest. We have been practising our presentation, and have discussed what we are going to wear and how we will stand. We have rehearsed the presentation until the timing and delivery are perfect. This process has increased everyone's confidence.'

After the presentation, Lara summed up the experience: 'I am happy to say that the presentation went like a dream all because we listened to the advice we were given.'

TOP TIP

Never read from prepared prompt cards! Look at the audience when you're talking and smile occasionally. If you need to use prompt cards as a reminder, write clearly so that you need only glance at them.

TOP TIP

Remember, the audience always makes allowances for some nerves!

Activity: Presentation true or false

Farida and Lauren have been asked to give a presentation on a visit they made to a local company. Think about the preparation, organisation and delivery of their presentation and decide whether the following statements are **True** or **False**. Circle your chosen answer.

a) Farida and Lauren should wait before starting on their presentation as they will forget things if they start too early. **True** **False**

b) They should discuss what they have to do and how long it will take. **True** **False**

c) They shouldn't divide up the work; they should both do the same work. **True** **False**

d) They shouldn't take into account their individual strengths and weaknesses. **True** **False**

e) The girls should decide on which visual aids are best to use for this topic. **True** **False**

f) They shouldn't consider handouts. **True** **False**

g) They shouldn't anticipate questions that they may be asked. **True** **False**

h) They should look at the audience when talking and smile occasionally. **True** **False**

i) They should not use prompt cards. **True** **False**

j) They should prepare thoroughly for the presentation. **True** **False**

k) It is perfectly normal for Farida and Lauren to feel nervous before the presentation. **True** **False**

l) It would be better not to take a few deep breaths before starting the presentation. **True** **False**

m) Farida and Lauren shouldn't bother checking their slides for errors – the audience will understand. **True** **False**

n) They should practise their presentation until they get it right. **True** **False**

o) They should not allow people to ask questions during the presentation. **True** **False**

p) Farida and Lauren should speak clearly and project their voices. **True** **False**

Your assessments

The importance of assignments

All learners on BTEC First courses are assessed by means of **assignments**. Each one is designed to link to specific **learning outcomes** and **grading criteria**. At the end of the course, your assignment grades put together determine your overall grade.

To get the best grade you can, you need to know the golden rules that apply to all assignments, then how to interpret the specific instructions.

10 golden rules for assignments

1 Check that you understand the instructions.

2 Check whether you have to do all the work on your own, or if you will do some as a member of a group. If you work as a team, you need to identify which parts are your own contributions.

3 Always write down any verbal instructions you are given.

4 Check the final deadline and any penalties for not meeting it.

5 Make sure you know what to do if you have a serious personal problem, eg illness, and need an official extension.

6 Copying someone else's work (**plagiarism**) is a serious offence and is easy for experienced tutors to spot. It's never worth the risk.

7 Schedule enough time for finding out the information and doing initial planning.

8 Allow plenty of time between talking to your tutor about your plans, preparations and drafts and the final deadline.

9 Don't panic if the assignment seems long or complicated. Break it down into small, manageable chunks.

10 If you suddenly get stuck, ask your tutor to talk things through with you.

Activity: Golden rules for assignments

This activity will test your understanding of the golden rules for tackling assignments. Each question has three statements; you have to decide which statement is correct. Place a tick next to the correct statement.

1 Before starting an assignment you should:

a) check that you understand the chapter in the textbook

b) check that you understand the assignment instructions

c) check that other people understand the instructions.

2 Before starting an assignment you should remember to:

a) write down what your friends say about the assignment

b) write down what other people say about the assignment
c) write down any verbal instructions you are given by your tutor.

3 When writing your assignment you should:
a) never copy other people's work
b) never put your own thoughts into the assignment
c) never read articles and journals.

4 When completing your assignments you should:
a) schedule your time carefully so that you can find out enough information
b) schedule plenty of time for your own enjoyment
c) schedule plenty of time to play computer games with your friends.

5 When writing your assignments, if you find that you do not understand something, you should:
a) not answer this part of the assignment
b) go and see the tutor to talk things through
c) write anything so that there is some form of answer.

Interpreting the instructions

Most assignments start with a **command word** – describe, explain, evaluate, etc. These words relate to how complex the answer should be.

Command words

Learners often don't do their best because they read the command words but don't understand exactly what they have to do. These tables show you what is required for each grade when you see a particular command word.

Command words and obtaining a pass

Complete ...	Complete a form, diagram or drawing.
Demonstrate ...	Show that you can do a particular activity.
Describe ...	Give a clear, straightforward description that includes all the main points.
Identify ...	Give all the basic facts relating to a certain topic.
List ...	Write a list of the main items (not sentences).
Name ...	State the proper terms related to a drawing or diagram.
Outline ...	Give all the main points, but without going into too much detail.
State ...	Point out or list the main features.

Examples:

- **List** the main features on your mobile phone.
- **Describe** the best way to greet a customer.
- **Outline** the procedures you follow to keep your computer system secure.

Command words and obtaining a merit

Analyse ...	Identify the factors that apply, and state how these are linked and how each of them relates to the topic.
Comment on ...	Give your own opinions or views.
Compare ... **Contrast ...**	Identify the main factors relating to two or more items and point out the similarities and differences.
Competently use ...	Take full account of information and feedback you have obtained to review or improve an activity.
Demonstrate ...	Prove you can carry out a more complex activity.
Describe ...	Give a full description including details of all the relevant features.
Explain ...	Give logical reasons to support your views.
Justify ...	Give reasons for the points you are making so that the reader knows what you're thinking.
Suggest ...	Give your own ideas or thoughts.

Examples:

- **Explain** why mobile phones are so popular.
- **Describe** the needs of four different types of customers.
- **Suggest** the type of procedures your employer would need to introduce to keep the IT system secure.

Command words and obtaining a distinction

Analyse ...	Identify several relevant factors, show how they are linked, and explain the importance of each.
Compare ... **Contrast ...**	Identify the main factors in two or more situations, then explain the similarities and differences, and in some cases say which is best and why.
Demonstrate ...	Prove that you can carry out a complex activity taking into account information you have obtained or received to adapt your original idea.
Describe ...	Give a comprehensive description which tells a story to the reader and shows that you can apply your knowledge and information correctly.
Evaluate ...	Bring together all your information and make a judgement on the importance or success of something.
Explain ...	Provide full details and reasons to support the arguments you are making.
Justify ...	Give full reasons or evidence to support your opinion.
Recommend ...	Weigh up all the evidence to come to a conclusion, with reasons, about what would be best.

Examples:

- **Evaluate** the features and performance of your mobile phone.
- **Analyse** the role of customer service in contributing to an organisation's success.
- **Justify** the main features on the website of a large, successful organisation of your choice.

TRY THIS

Check the command word you are likely to see for each of your units in the **grading grid** in advance. This tells you the **grading criteria** for the unit so that you know the evidence you will have to present.

TOP TIP

Think of assignments as an opportunity to demonstrate what you've learnt and to get useful feedback on your work.

Case study: Interpreting command words

Liam is getting ready to begin an assignment and starts by reading the task brief. He realises that he does not understand what one of the instructions means. As this is an individual assignment, he knows that he has to do all the work on his own. He also knows that the assignment has to be submitted in three weeks' time. Liam decides that he needs to talk to his tutor the next day so that he can ask about the instruction that isn't clear.

Following the meeting with his tutor, Liam begins to plan how he is going to obtain the information he needs and he sets a date for starting to write his first draft. He begins by breaking the assignment down into smaller bite-size chunks, which makes the whole project easier to manage.

When Liam starts his research by looking on the internet, he finds some very useful articles. Liam remembers what his tutor has told him about copying other people's work (plagiarism) and makes notes using his own words.

The first task asks Liam 'to describe different types of businesses' and covers the pass performance criterion. Liam looks at the table in his Study Skills Guide to make sure he knows what this means.

The second task covers the merit criterion and asks Liam to 'analyse' a particular situation. Again, he looks up what this means before attempting the task. He discovers that 'analyse' means identifying the factors that apply in this situation, stating how each factor relates to the topic and saying how they are linked to each other.

The third task covers the distinction criterion and asks Liam to 'evaluate', which he already knows means to bring together all the information and make a judgement on the issues being explored. Liam attempts the distinction criteria but finds this task quite hard.

By the time Liam attempts his third assignment, he has become very familiar with the variety of command words being used and finds that he no longer has to refer to his Study Skills Guide to find out what they mean.

Activity: Assignments – following instructions

This activity reviews your ability to interpret instructions.

1 Answer each question below, concentrating on what the command word is actually telling you to do.

a) Describe the clothes you are wearing.

b) Name the companies that make your clothes.

c) Compare the adverts of your two favourite products.

d) Suggest how you might improve a clothing brand you don't like.

e) Explain why it is important to dress smartly when you go for an interview.

f) Analyse why teenagers like to dress cool.

2 The next part of the activity reviews your knowledge of pass, merit and distinction criteria. There are three questions below which all cover the same topic. One has been set at pass level, one at merit and one at distinction. Try to answer the questions, focusing on the command words at the beginning.

Pass

a) Describe the two retail superstores, Asda and Sainsbury's.

Merit

b) Compare the two retail superstores Asda and Sainsbury's.

Distinction

c) Evaluate why these retail giants are two of the leaders in the grocery superstore market.

Having attempted these questions, you can see that, as you move from pass to merit to distinction, the questions become harder to answer. Merit and distinction levels require greater understanding and more analysis of the issues being explored.

Sample assignment

Note about assignments

All learners are different and will approach their assignments in different ways. The sample assignment that follows shows how one learner answered a brief to achieve pass, merit and distinction level criteria. The learner's work shows just one way in which these grading criteria can be evidenced. There are no standard or set answers. If you produce the required evidence for each task then you will achieve the grading criteria covered by the assignment.

Sample assignment front sheet

A completed front sheet must be submitted. This allows your tutor to identify clearly the work you are submitting and that it is your own.

Assignments must be submitted by the completion date. Please refer to your centre's submission policy on late work.

Your tutor will be more than happy to give you feedback on your assignment progress to date, before submitting a version for assessment.

This front sheet must be completed by the learner where appropriate and included with the work submitted for assessment.

Learner name	Assessor name
Jason Evans	Mr J Morris

Date issued	Completion date	Submitted on
12 November 2010	10 December 2010	7 December 2010

Qualification	Unit
BTEC Level 2 First Diploma in Business	Unit 1: Business Purposes

Assignment title	Contrasting business purposes and types of ownership

In this assessment you will have opportunities to provide evidence against the following criteria. Indicate the page numbers where the evidence can be found.

Criteria reference	To achieve the criteria the evidence must show that the student is able to:	Task no.	Page numbers
P1	identify the purpose of four different business organisations	1	1
P2	describe the different types of business ownership, linking this to the size and scale of four different organisations	2	2
M1	contrast the ownership and purposes of two different business organisations	3	3
D1	evaluate how a business organisation has responded to changes in the business environment	4	4

Learner declaration

I certify that the work submitted for this assignment is my own and research sources are fully acknowledged.

Learner signature: *Jason Evans* Date: *7 December 2010*

This table is very important as it indicates the assessment criterion that is being covered in the particular task.

You must never take someone's words or ideas and use them as if they were your own, unless you indicate clearly in your work where you obtained this information.

The evidence that you provide can take many different forms for Business, such as formal reports, evaluations, notes, verbal recordings, question and answer sessions, logbooks, plans, observations and presentations.

Sample assignment brief

Your assignments will usually begin with a scenario that gives the work a vocational setting.

Always keep focused on the title, as this will help you to keep to the requirements of the assignment tasks.

Unit title	Unit 1: Business Purposes
Qualification	BTEC Level 2 First Diploma in Business
Start date	12 November 2010
Deadline date	10 December 2010
Assessor	Mr J Morris

Assignment title	Contrasting business purposes and types of ownership

The purpose of this assignment is to:
allow you to demonstrate your knowledge and understanding of the ownership of different businesses, their purposes and how they have responded to change.

Scenario
You work for a local enterprise agency that produces a monthly magazine. You have been asked to write an article for the magazine. By completing the following four tasks you should be able to produce the article as required.

Task 1
You will find that there are many different businesses in your area, each pursuing different purposes. Select four business organisations in your local area by choosing:

- a public sector organisation such as a school or the local authority
- a local charity
- a large private sector business
- a small private sector business.

Research and identify the purposes of each of the four organisations. This will form the introduction to your magazine article.

This provides evidence for P1

Task 2
You now have information about four local organisations, each with a different type of ownership. Describe how each of these organisations is owned and link your descriptions to the size and scale of each organisation. In other words, describe whether they are small, medium or large organisations and whether they operate locally, regionally, nationally, across Europe or throughout the world. Your descriptions of ownership, size and scale can be given in the form of a table, to be included in the body of your magazine article.

This provides evidence for P2

Task 3
The next part of the article deals with the differences that exist between two of your organisations in terms of ownership and purpose. Select one organisation that operates in the private sector and one organisation that operates either in the public sector or in the voluntary sector (as a charity). Compare these two organisations in terms of their ownership and business purposes. Your observations will form the next part of the article.

This provides evidence for M1

Task 4
For the final part of the article select one of the two organisations you have chosen for Task 3. Evaluate how it has responded to changes in its business environment. Your evaluation should include a judgement on whether you think it has responded well or poorly to those changes. For example, supermarkets are now staying open longer, sometimes all night, and have expanded their range of products, which they will argue is in response to customer needs. This final part of the article allows you to consider in depth the reasons behind any changes made by your chosen business.

This provides evidence for D1

'Identify' means to give the key elements, facts, features, etc. of something.

'Compare' means to examine and note the similarities and differences between two or more things.

'Evaluate' means to make a judgement on the value, quality or importance of something, and whether you think it is successful.

'Describe' means to provide information that includes relevant features, characteristics, facts, etc.

These resources will help you to understand the information and concepts included in the assignment.

Sources of information

Books

Carysforth C and Neild M — ***BTEC First Business*** (Heinemann, 2004) ISBN 0435401386

Fardon M, Nuttall C and Prokopiw J — ***GCSE Applied Business*** (Osborne Books, 2002) ISBN

Websites

www.businesslink.gov.uk The Business Link site provides information about business and local economic conditions

www.thetimes100.co.uk The Times 100 case studies

www.bized.co.uk A business education resource site

www.bbc.co.uk See the business pages of the BBC website

www.canterbury.gov.uk/buildpage.php?id=3225 This is an example of a local business support website

This brief has beeen verified as being fit for purpose			
Assessor	Mr J Morris		
Signature	*J Morris*	Date	*11 October 2010*
Internal verifier	Ms A Cooke		
Signature	*Angela Cooke*	Date	*11 October 2010*

Sample learner work

This investigation should enhance your understanding of the similarities and differences between very large and small businesses. It contributes well to P1.

Sample learner work: page 1

Contrasting business purposes and types of ownership

Task 1 (P1)

Range of purposes of local businesses

This article looks at four businesses that are based locally, some of which are only found in this area, while others have a branch locally but operate over a much wider area.

The first business is Tesco plc, which operate in the profit-making private sector and have a large local supermarket. Their purpose is to sell grocery products and non-foods to the public and to make a profit.

The second local business belongs to my uncle and he is a sole trader. His business is called D Williams (Plumbing Services). He employs three other people who help him repair plumbing problems. They operate locally and the firm earns enough to pay the wages of everyone and make a

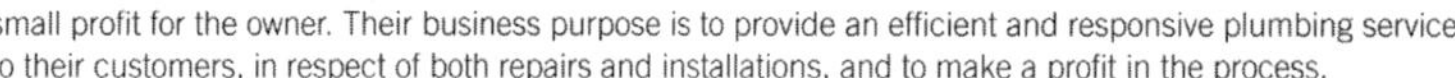

small profit for the owner. Their business purpose is to provide an efficient and responsive plumbing service to their customers, in respect of both repairs and installations, and to make a profit in the process.

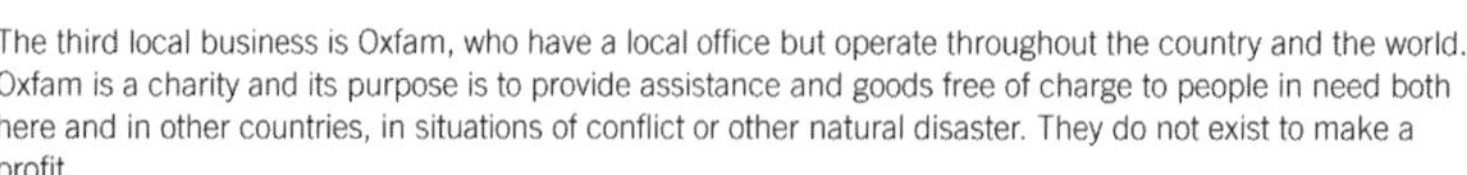

The third local business is Oxfam, who have a local office but operate throughout the country and the world. Oxfam is a charity and its purpose is to provide assistance and goods free of charge to people in need both here and in other countries, in situations of conflict or other natural disaster. They do not exist to make a profit.

The fourth business is Mid and West Wales Fire and Rescue Service. The Mid and West Wales Fire and Rescue Service is a public sector organisation funded directly by its six local government authorities. The fire service's purpose is to make the local community safe and to prevent injury and death from fire. It receives funding from the local authorities, which allows them to employ fire officers and maintain and buy fire-fighting equipment. It is non-profit-making.

The choice of Oxfam and Tesco plc is good because they are found worldwide but also have a local presence. Performance criterion P1 is achieved.

This is a good summary of the ownership of Tesco plc which is typical of very large plcs. It contributes to the achievement of P2.

The learner has shown good understanding of the liability issues associated with sole traders, providing effective evidence for P2.

Again, a good summary emphasising the size and scale of Tesco plc, contributing effectively to P2.

Sample learner work: page 2

Task 2 (P2)

Ownership of local businesses

Business	Ownership	Size	Scale of operation
Tesco plc	Tesco plc is a very large business and is a public limited company (plc). Its shares are traded on the stock exchange and can be owned by the public. By selling shares to the public Tesco can raise large amounts of money to grow the business. It has an authorised share capital of at least £50,000 and is registered at Companies House as a plc. Therefore anyone who owns shares in Tesco plc is a part owner of the business.	Tesco plc is a very large business.	Tesco plc is the fourth largest retailer in the world, employing over 200,000 people worldwide. They operate in over 30 countries and are expanding all the time. They are a European, and rapidly becoming a global, company.
D Williams (Plumbing Services)	This business is known as a sole trader. A sole trader describes any business that is owned and controlled by one person, although they may employ workers. The owners are **personally liable** for the firm's debts, and may have to pay them out of their own pocket. It is a profit-making business operating in the private sector.	D Williams (Plumbing Services) is a small business.	This business only operates within the South West Wales area.
Oxfam	Oxfam is a registered charity, which is funded by donations from the public and other bodies. Trustees run the charity and they rely on fundraising and keeping their administrative costs low. For each £1 invested in attracting and maintaining financial support, they try to get at least £6 in income. They are accountable to the Charity Commission and its regulations. They are also accountable to governments in countries where they operate. It is non-profit-making.	Oxfam is a large organisation, having thousands of staff and volunteers all over the world.	Oxfam is a global business operating throughout the world
The Mid and West Wales Fire and Rescue Service	The local governments in the area in which it operates own this business. They fund the service. This is a public sector, non-profit-making business. The Fire Service uses its funding to pay its staff and maintain and replace fire-fighting equipment.	The Mid and West Wales Fire and Rescue Service is a large business employing 1400 staff.	The fire service is a regional operation serving Mid and West Wales only.

A clear explanation of the ownership of Oxfam, showing how very different a charity is in terms of ownership, indicating good understanding of the requirements of P2.

An interesting choice for a public sector organisation, showing good understanding of this type of ownership and contributing to P2.

This organisation covers a huge geographic area, which has a very low population. The learner has achieved this performance criterion – P2.

The learner's choice of organisations to compare will allow investigation of the types of ownership and purposes in quite some depth, helping to demonstrate evidence for M1.

The learner has explained the differing purposes between the two organisations very well, demonstrating evidence for M1.

Sample learner work: page 3

Task 3 (M1)

Local ownership and purposes compared

It is interesting to compare two of the selected businesses in terms of their differing ownership and purposes. For the purpose of such comparison, we will look at Tesco plc and the Mid and West Wales Fire Service.

The ownership of these two businesses is very different as Tesco plc is a profit-making business and can be owned by anyone who is able to buy shares in the company. This is not the case with the Fire Service, as the public cannot directly own the service. It is owned by the six local authorities that give money to the service in order for it to operate. Indirectly, you could argue that because the public in these areas pays council tax and other taxes, which go to fund the local authorities, then the public do in a sense own their local fire service. In practice the public cannot own all the shares in Tesco plc, and cannot therefore be said to 'own' Tesco plc.

Tesco exist to make a profit, whereas the fire service does not. They both have very different purposes; Tesco's principal purpose is to supply goods and services at a profit. Sometimes if they have too much stock in a particular line, or if it isn't selling, the company will change their purpose for that product and sell at cost or below cost, incurring a loss in order to get rid of the product. The fire service's purpose is to make safe, sustainable communities, where avoidable deaths, injuries and damage from fire and other emergencies are minimised, and their funding from the local authorities is allocated accordingly (www.mawwfire.gov.uk/about_eng/vision.asp). The fire service therefore provides a service to the public, but not to make a profit.

Tesco's purposes are embedded within their overall objectives, which according to the company's website are:

- to be a successful international retailer
- to grow the core UK business
- to be as strong in non-food as in food
- to develop retailing services, such as Tesco Personal Finance, Telecoms and Tesco.com
- to put community at the heart of what we do.

See www.tescoplc.com/plc/about_us/strategy/.

The Fire Service has very different aims, and therefore different purposes also, to Tesco plc. The following is taken from the Mid and West Wales Fire Service website:

1. To save lives and protect communities.
2. To be trusted and respected by our communities.
3. To be seen as more than an emergency service.
4. To manage within budget.
5. To make efficiencies year on year.
6. To match our resources to priorities.
7. To seek out and utilise alternative resources.
8. To manage our people effectively.
9. To fully develop risk reduction planning.
10. To develop effective partnership working.
11. To develop our workforce into effective and empowered people.

See www.mawwfire.gov.uk/about_eng/vision.asp.

All this has to be achieved within the financial limits of the money they have been given.

A clear concise summary of Tesco's purposes, contributing to M1.

Again a good summary of the fire service's purposes, completing the requirement for criterion M1.

It may have been appropriate here to have discussed the various store formats that Tesco has developed.

A good summary of how Tesco plc has experienced change and how the business is responding, effectively contributing to D1.

The learner has discussed some very interesting points here, highlighting how important it is for Tesco to be constantly adjusting its business to changes in its environment. This contributes to the achievement of D1.

Sample learner work: page 4

Task 4 (D1)

Tesco's responses to changes in its business environment

Tesco plc's website (www.tescoplc.com/plc/) states that Tesco is a global business operating in the grocery, non-food and clothing markets. Their core UK business has over 280,000 employees and over 2,100 stores.

There have been many changes in Tesco's business environment over the last 40 years. Customers are now more mobile and possess cars. Tesco has responded to this by developing huge out of town Tesco Extra stores which have large car parks. This was also made possible by the government allowing them planning permission to build. Customers now want one-stop shopping. Tesco has responded by making sure its stores stock nearly everything a customer might want. Over the last 40 years people have travelled abroad a lot more and have tried different foods. Tesco has responded by increasing its range of foreign foods such as Mexican, Indian and Chinese. The large ethnic populations that have moved to the UK have also made Tesco respond by increasing its range of foods.

When microwaves were launched and people started buying them, Tesco responded by introducing a range of microwaveable foods. Tesco has responded to people wishing to eat healthier by making sure their products are healthy and by putting advice labels on the packets. Customers have wanted to shop more conveniently to fit in with their lifestyles; Tesco has responded by trading at more convenient times, including offering 24-hour shopping and opening for six hours on Sundays.

Many people now do not want to eat food that has been grown or reared using chemicals, they want natural food. Tesco has responded by introducing organic food ranges. Customers want a clean pleasant place to shop and Tesco has responded by making their shops light and attractive. The government wants everyone to be environmentally aware; Tesco has responded by increasing the amount of recyclable packaging that is used for its products. Tesco are also reducing the number of free plastic bags they give away and are also reducing the size of each store's carbon footprint. They have built small neighbourhood stores – Tesco Express – to respond to customers' desire to shop conveniently locally. Tesco has responded to local needs by helping with community projects, for example the 'computers for schools' project. They have also responded to the increasing number of people wishing to work flexibly by offering employment, which allows people to work around their family commitments.

Tesco has responded to laws that have changed the business environment, such as food labelling laws and consumer protection laws, by leading the way in putting the customer first. Tesco are always conducting research to identify changes in the business environment and then responding to the customer needs that its research identifies. Sometimes the company is criticised for not reacting positively to changes in the business environment. Tesco has grown enormously and has forced many small retailers out of business; they have received a lot of criticism in this area and appear not to care. They have also been criticised for the low prices they pay UK farmers for their products, which in some cases has forced farms to close. They have responded to growing customer demand for more regular shopping visits and a greater range of product by developing very large out of town hypermarkets. Customers travel further to get to such stores, which doesn't help the environment, however online shopping has countered this by encouraging many customers to reduce the number of visits they pay to Tesco stores.

Although Tesco has been criticised for not responding to the needs of some of its stakeholders, such as UK farmers, and by those who think they are not doing enough to reduce binge drinking among young people, they have generally responded well to changes in their business environment. This evaluation has considered how they have responded to external changes such as the way people live, political issues, economic issues and technological developments. In evaluating or judging how well they have responded, I think they have responded well to external changes concerning their customers but not so well in a small number of other areas where change has occurred and negatively affected some of their other stakeholders.

A very good account of how Tesco plc has responded to changes which are not always in every stakeholder's interest, clearly evaluating these changes for D1.

D1 fully achieved.

Highlighting responses that Tesco has made which are not in some groups' interests contributes to the overall evaluation for D1.

Sample assessor's comments

Here you have the chance to say whether you agree with the feedback given by the assessor. This is an important part of the assessment process.

This column indicates whether you have met the performance criteria. 'Y' means you have, 'N' means that you have not.

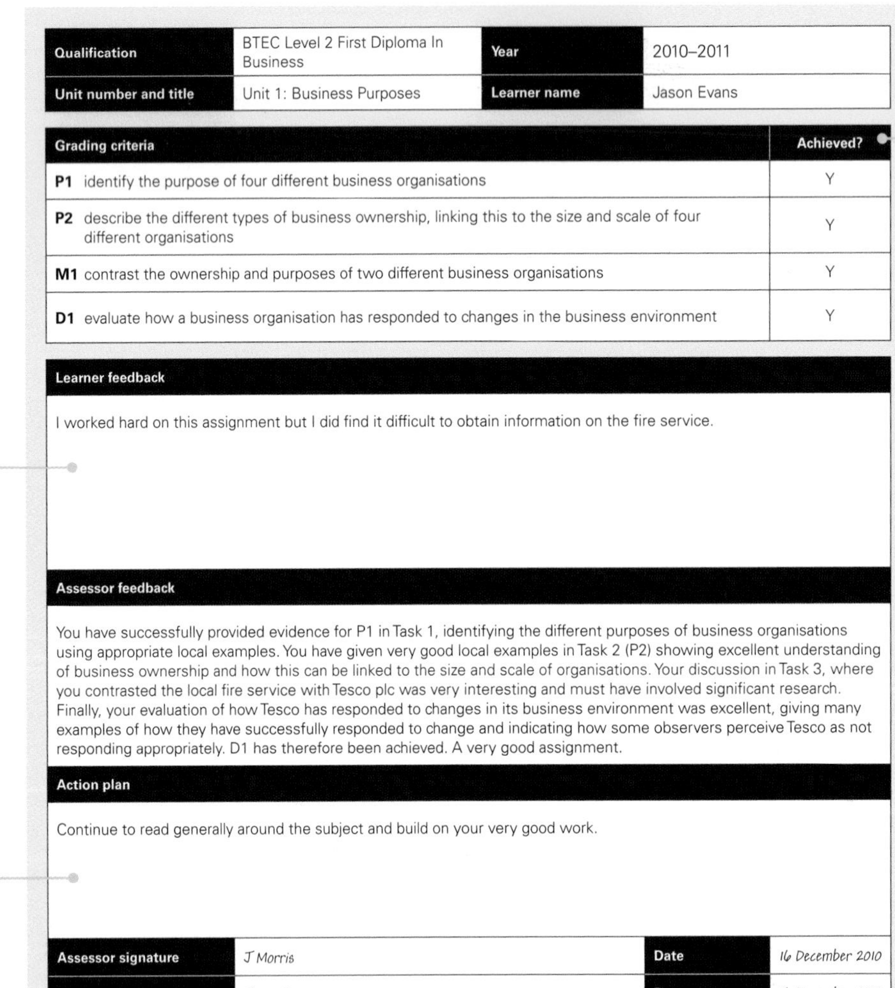

Qualification	BTEC Level 2 First Diploma In Business	Year	2010–2011
Unit number and title	Unit 1: Business Purposes	Learner name	Jason Evans

Grading criteria	Achieved?
P1 identify the purpose of four different business organisations	Y
P2 describe the different types of business ownership, linking this to the size and scale of four different organisations	Y
M1 contrast the ownership and purposes of two different business organisations	Y
D1 evaluate how a business organisation has responded to changes in the business environment	Y

Learner feedback

I worked hard on this assignment but I did find it difficult to obtain information on the fire service.

Assessor feedback

You have successfully provided evidence for P1 in Task 1, identifying the different purposes of business organisations using appropriate local examples. You have given very good local examples in Task 2 (P2) showing excellent understanding of business ownership and how this can be linked to the size and scale of organisations. Your discussion in Task 3, where you contrasted the local fire service with Tesco plc was very interesting and must have involved significant research. Finally, your evaluation of how Tesco has responded to changes in its business environment was excellent, giving many examples of how they have successfully responded to change and indicating how some observers perceive Tesco as not responding appropriately. D1 has therefore been achieved. A very good assignment.

Action plan

Continue to read generally around the subject and build on your very good work.

Assessor signature	J Morris	Date	16 December 2010
Learner signature	Jason Evans	Date	16 December 2010

The action planning process is essential as this plan clearly indicates what you need to do to improve your work in the future.

Coping with problems

Most learners sail through their BTEC First with no major problems. Unfortunately, not everyone is so lucky. Some may have personal difficulties or other issues that disrupt their work so they are late handing in their assignments. If this happens to you, it's vital to know what to do. This checklist should help.

Checklist for coping with problems

- ✔ Check that you know who to talk to.
- ✔ Don't sit on a problem and worry about it. Talk to someone promptly, in confidence. It's always easier to cope if you've shared it with someone.
- ✔ Most centres have professional counsellors you can talk to if you prefer. They won't repeat anything you say to them without your permission.
- ✔ If you've done something wrong or silly, people will respect you more if you are honest, admit where you went wrong and apologise promptly.

Case study: Talking about problems

For the first term and a half Gemma has been performing well in the BTEC First, but she is having trouble understanding what the current unit is all about. She has always been a little overwhelmed by financial information.

She is reluctant to tell others in the class about her fear of figures, as they all seem to grasp the topic, and she is embarrassed to discuss it with her tutor. From the first lesson she struggles to comprehend what is being taught and, as finance tends to build on what has been delivered in the previous lessons, she soon falls behind.

The first assignment is due in two weeks and she is worried that it will be impossible to obtain a pass with her current level of understanding. She discusses the situation with her parents. They are unable to help with the course work but tell her to talk to the unit tutor as soon as possible. Eventually, Gemma plucks up enough courage to talk to the tutor. He tells her that her one-to-one tutorial, which is scheduled for tomorrow, will be dedicated to ensuring she understands the finance parts of the unit.

The tutorial is a success and, for the first time, Gemma begins to grasp the basic concepts. The tutor gives her some easier financial examples for homework and tells her to see him the next day to discuss how she got on. She manages to complete the tasks successfully and now feels more confident about tackling the assignment.

The tutor said, 'I wish Gemma had come to see me earlier. I think learners sometimes feel embarrassed about talking to tutors if they don't grasp parts of the course. That's what I am here for; to ensure that learners understand the new skills and are able to apply them.'

TOP TIP

If you have a serious complaint or concern, talk to your chosen tutor first – for example if you believe an assignment grade is unfair. All centres have official procedures to cover important issues such as appeals about assignments and formal complaints but it's usually sensible to try to resolve a problem informally first.

Activity: Coping with problems

Below are some statements about learners who are experiencing problems and three possible alternatives for dealing with each problem. Indicate which alternative is most appropriate for dealing with that problem.

1 Leroy has a problem understanding what a particular instruction in an assignment means. Should he:
   a) ask his friends what it means?
   b) ask his tutor what it means?
   c) ask his parents what it means?

2 Amy has a difficult personal problem, which isn't health related, and she feels she cannot discuss it with her tutor. Should she:
   a) talk to another tutor?
   b) talk to a doctor?
   c) talk to the college counsellor?

3 David is very confused and stressed about what job he could do in the future. Should he:
   a) contact some local employers?
   b) look at newspaper jobs adverts?
   c) make an appointment to see the careers adviser?

4 Tammy has done something silly; she has copied her assignment from another classmate and now feels guilty about it. What should she do?
   a) If she is found out, claim that the other learner copied her?
   b) Talk to the tutor, tell the truth and apologise?
   c) Say nothing and hope the tutor doesn't notice?

5 Tomas has just received his marked assignment back and is disappointed as he has been awarded a pass grade. He did spend a lot of time on the assignment and, as far as he can make out, all the merit criteria have been met. Should he:
   a) talk to his tutor?
   b) complain to the head teacher or principal?
   c) ask his parents to write a letter?

Skills building

To do your best in your assignments you need a number of skills, including:

- your **personal, learning and thinking skills**
- your **functional skills** of ICT, mathematics and English
- your proofreading and document-production skills.

Personal, learning and thinking skills (PLTS)

These are the skills, personal qualities and behaviour that you find in people who are effective and confident at work. These people enjoy carrying out a wide range of tasks, always try to do their best and work well alone or with others. They enjoy a challenge and use new experiences to learn and develop.

Activity: How good are your PLTS?

1 Do this quiz to help you identify areas for improvement.

a) I get on well with other people.

Always **Usually** **Seldom** **Never**

b) I try to find out other people's suggestions for solving problems that puzzle me.

Always **Usually** **Seldom** **Never**

c) I plan carefully to make sure I meet my deadlines.

Always **Usually** **Seldom** **Never**

d) If someone is being difficult, I think carefully before making a response.

Always **Usually** **Seldom** **Never**

e) I don't mind sharing my possessions or my time.

Always **Usually** **Seldom** **Never**

f) I take account of other people's views and opinions.

Always **Usually** **Seldom** **Never**

g) I enjoy thinking of new ways of doing things.

Always **Usually** **Seldom** **Never**

h) I like creating new and different things.

Always **Usually** **Seldom** **Never**

i) I enjoy planning and finding ways of solving problems.

Always **Usually** **Seldom** **Never**

j) I enjoy getting feedback about my performance.

Always **Usually** **Seldom** **Never**

k) I try to learn from constructive criticism so that I know what to improve.

Always **Usually** **Seldom** **Never**

l) I enjoy new challenges.

Always **Usually** **Seldom** **Never**

m) I am even-tempered.

Always **Usually** **Seldom** **Never**

n) I am happy to make changes when necessary.

Always **Usually** **Seldom** **Never**

o) I like helping other people.

Always **Usually** **Seldom** **Never**

Score 3 points for each time you answered 'Always', 2 points for 'Usually', 1 point for 'Seldom' and 0 points for 'Never'. The higher your score, the higher your personal, learning and thinking skills.

2 How creative are you? Test yourself with this activity. Identify 50 different objects you could fit into a matchbox at the same time! As a start, three suitable items are a postage stamp, a grain of rice, a staple. Can you find 47 more?

Functional skills

Functional skills are the practical skills you need to function confidently, effectively and independently at work, when studying and in everyday life. They focus on the following areas:

- Information and Communications Technology (ICT)
- Maths
- English.

You may already be familiar with functional skills. Your BTEC First tutors will give you more information about how you will continue to develop these skills on your new course.

BTEC FACT

Your BTEC First qualification is at Level 2. Qualifications in functional skills start at Entry level and continue to Level 2. (You don't need to achieve functional skills to gain any BTEC qualification and the evidence from a BTEC assignment can't be used towards the assessment of functional skills.)

ICT skills

These will relate directly to how much 'hands-on' practice you have had on IT equipment. You may be an experienced IT user and using word processing, spreadsheet and presentation software may be second nature. Searching for information online may be something you do every day – in between downloading music, buying or selling on eBay and updating your Facebook profile!

Or you may prefer to avoid computer contact as much as possible. If so, there are two things you need to do.

1 Use every opportunity to improve your ICT skills so that you can start to live in the 21st century!
2 Make life easier by improving your basic proofreading and document preparation skills.

Proofreading and document preparation skills

Being able to produce well-displayed work quickly will make your life a lot easier. On any course there will be at least one unit that requires you to use good document preparation skills.

Tips to improve your document production skills

- ✔ If your keyboarding skills are poor, ask if there is a workshop you can join. Or your library or resource centre may have software you can use.
- ✔ Check that you know the format of documents you have to produce for assignments. It can help to have a 'model' version of each type in your folder for quick reference.
- ✔ Practise checking your work by reading word by word – and remember not to rely on spellcheckers (see page 57).

TRY THIS

Learning to touch type can save you hours of time. To check your keyboarding skills go to www.pearsonhotlinks.co.uk, insert the express code 5780S and click on the link for this page.

TOP TIP

Print your work on good paper and keep it flat so that it looks good when you hand it in.

Activity: How good are your ICT skills?

1a) Test your current ICT abilities by responding *honestly* to each of the following statements.

i) I can create a copy of my timetable using a word-processing or spreadsheet package.
True **False**

ii) I can devise and design a budget for myself for the next three months using a spreadsheet package.
True **False**

iii) I can email a friend who has just got broadband to say how to minimise the danger of computer viruses, what a podcast is and also explain the restrictions on music downloads.
True **False**

iv) I can use presentation software to prepare a presentation containing four or five slides on a topic of my choice.
True **False**

v) I can research online to compare the performance and prices of laptop computers and prepare an information sheet using word-processing software.
True **False**

vi) I can prepare a poster, with graphics, for my mother's friend, who is starting her own business preparing children's party food, and attach it to an email to her for approval.
True **False**

1b) Select any one of the above to which you answered false and learn how to do it.

2 Compare the two tables below. The first is an original document; the second is a typed copy. Are they identical? Highlight any differences you find and check them with the key on page 89.

Name	Date	Time	Room
Abbott	16 July	9.30 am	214
Grey	10 August	10.15 am	160
Johnston	12 August	2.20 pm	208
Waverley	18 July	3.15 pm	180
Jackson	30 September	11.15 am	209
Gregory	31 August	4.20 pm	320
Marshall	10 September	9.30 am	170
Bradley	16 September	2.20 pm	210

Name	Date	Time	Room
Abbott	26 July	9.30 am	214
Gray	10 August	10.15 am	160
Johnson	12 August	2.20 pm	208
Waverley	18 July	3.15 am	180
Jackson	31 September	11.15 am	209
Gregory	31 August	4.20 pm	320
Marshall	10 September	9.30 pm	170
Bradley	16 August	2.20 pm	201

Maths or numeracy skills

Four easy ways to improve your numeracy skills

1 Work out simple calculations in your head, like adding up the prices of items you are buying. Then check if you are correct when you pay for them.

2 Set yourself numeracy problems based on your everyday life. For example, if you are on a journey that takes 35 minutes and you leave home at 11.10am, what time will you arrive? If you are travelling at 40 miles an hour, how long will it take you to go 10 miles?

3 Treat yourself to a Maths Training program.

4 Check out online sites to improve your skills. Go to www.pearsonhotlinks.co.uk, insert the express code 5780S and click on the link for this page.

TOP TIP

Quickly test answers. For example, if fuel costs 85p a litre and someone is buying 15 litres, estimate this at £1 x 15 (£15) and the answer should be just below this. So if your answer came out at £140, you'd immediately know you'd done something wrong!

Activity: How good are your maths skills?

Answer as many of the following questions as you can in 15 minutes. Check your answers with the key on page 89.

1 a) 12 + 28 = ?

i) 30 ii) 34 iii) 38 iv) 40 v) 48

b) 49 ÷ 7 = ?

i) 6 ii) 7 iii) 8 iv) 9 v) 10

c) ½ + 1¼ = ?

i) ¾ ii) 1½ iii) 1¾ iv) 2¼ v) 3

d) 4 × 12 = 8 × ?

i) 5 ii) 6 iii) 7 iv) 8 v) 9

e) 16.5 + 25.25 – ? = 13.25

i) 28.5 ii) 31.25 iii) 34.5 iv) 41.65 v) 44

2 a) You buy four items at £1.99, two at 98p and three at £1.75. You hand over a £20 note. How much change will you get? ______________

b) What fraction of one litre is 250 ml? ______________

c) What percentage of £50 is £2.50? ______________

d) A designer travelling on business can claim 38.2p a mile in expenses. How much is she owed if she travels 625 miles? ______________

e) You are flying to New York in December. New York is five hours behind British time and the flight lasts eight hours. If you leave at 11.15 am, what time will you arrive? ______________

f) For your trip to the United States you need American dollars. You find that the exchange rate is $1.5 dollars.

i) How many dollars will you receive if you exchange £500? ________

ii) Last year your friend visited New York when the exchange rate was $1.8. She also exchanged £500. Did she receive more dollars than you or fewer – and by how much? ______________

g) A security guard and his dog patrol the perimeter fence of a warehouse each evening. The building is 480 metres long and 300 metres wide and the fence is 80 metres out from the building on all sides. If the guard and his dog patrol the fence three times a night, how far will they walk? ______________

English skills

BTEC FACT

Reading, writing, speaking and listening are all part of the Functional English qualifications.

Your English skills affect your ability to understand what you read, prepare a written document, say what you mean and understand other people. Even if you're doing a practical subject, there will always be times when you need to leave someone a note, tell them about a phone call, read or listen to instructions – or write a letter for a job application!

Six easy ways to improve your English skills

1. Read more. It increases the number of words you know and helps to make you familiar with correct spellings.
2. Look up words you don't understand in a dictionary and check their meaning. Then try to use them yourself to increase your vocabulary.
3. Do crosswords. These help increase your vocabulary and practise your spelling at the same time.
4. You can use websites to help you get to grips with English vocabulary, grammar and punctuation. Go to www.pearsonhotlinks.co.uk, insert the express code 5780S and click on the link for this page.
5. Welcome opportunities to practise speaking in class, in discussion groups and during presentations – rather than avoiding them!
6. Test your ability to listen to someone else by seeing how much you can remember when they've finished speaking.

TOP TIP

If someone you're talking to uses a word, phrase or abbreviation you don't know, ask them what it means.

Activity: How good are your English skills?

1 In the table below are 'wrong' versions of words often spelled incorrectly. Write the correct spellings on the right. Check your list against the answers on page 89.

Incorrect spelling	Correct spelling
accomodation	
seperate	
definate	
payed	
desparate	
acceptible	
competant	
succesful	

2 Correct the error(s) in these sentences.

a) The plug on the computer is lose.

b) The car was stationery outside the house.

c) Their going on they're holidays tomorrow.

d) The principle of the college is John Smith.

e) We are all going accept Tom.

3 Punctuate these sentences correctly.

a) Toms train was late on Monday and Tuesday.

b) She is going to France Belgium Spain and Italy in the summer.

c) He comes from Leeds and says its wgreat there.

4 Read the article on copyright.

Copyright

Anyone who uses a photocopier can break copyright law if they carry out unrestricted photocopying of certain documents. This is because The Copyright, Designs and Patents Act 1988 protects the creator of an original work against having it copied without permission.

Legally, every time anyone writes a book, composes a song, makes a film or creates any other type of artistic work, this work is treated as their property (or copyright). If anyone else wishes to make use of it, they must get permission to do so and, on occasions, pay a fee.

Licences can be obtained to allow educational establishments to photocopy limited numbers of some publications. In addition, copies of an original document can be made for certain specific purposes. These include research and private study. Under the Act, too, if an article is summarised and quoted by anyone, then the author and title of the original work must be acknowledged.

a) Test your ability to understand unfamiliar information by responding to the following statements with 'True' or 'False'.

i) Students and tutors in schools and colleges can copy anything they want.
True **False**

ii) The law which covers copyright is The Copyright, Designs and Patents Act 1988.
True **False**

iii) A student photocopying a document in the library must have a licence.
True **False**

iv) Copyright only relates to books in the library.
True **False**

v) If you quote a newspaper report in an assignment, you don't need to state the source.
True **False**

vii) Anyone is allowed to photocopy a page of a book for research purposes.
True **False**

b) Make a list of key points in the article, then write a brief summary in your own words.

5 Nikki has read a newspaper report that a horse racing in the Kentucky Derby had to be put down. The filly collapsed and the vet couldn't save her. Nikki says it's the third time in two years a racehorse has had to be put down in the US. As a horse lover she is convinced racing should be banned in Britain and the US. She argues that fox hunting was banned to protect foxes, and that racehorses are more important and more expensive than foxes. Darren disagrees. He says the law is not working, hardly anyone has been prosecuted and fox hunting is going on just like before. Debbie says that animals aren't important whilst there is famine in the world.

a) Do you think the three arguments are logical? See if you can spot the flaws and check your ideas with the suggestions on page 89.

b) Sporting activities and support for sporting teams often provoke strong opinions. For a sport or team of your choice, identify two opposing views that might be held. Then decide how you would give a balanced view. Test your ideas with a friend or family member.

Answers

Skills building answers

ICT activities

2 Differences between the two tables are highlighted in bold.

Name	Date	Time	Room
Abbott	**16** July	9.30 am	214
Grey	10 August	10.15 am	160
Johnston	12 August	2.20 pm	208
Waverley	18 July	3.15 **pm**	180
Jackson	**30** September	11.15 am	209
Gregory	31 August	4.20 pm	320
Marshall	10 September	9.30 **am**	170
Bradley	16 **September**	2.20 pm	**210**

Maths/numeracy activities

1 **a)** iv, **b)** ii, **c)** iii, **d)** ii, **e)** i

2 **a)** £4.83, **b)** ¼, **c)** 5%, **d)** £238.75, **e)** 2.15 pm, **f) i)** $750 **ii)** $150 dollars more, **g)** 6.6 km.

English activities

1 Spellings: accommodation, separate, definite, paid, desperate, acceptable, competent, successful

2 Errors:
a) The plug on the computer is loose.
b) The car was stationary outside the house.
c) They're going on their holidays tomorrow.
d) The principal of the college is John Smith.
e) We are all going except Tom.

3 Punctuation:
a) Tom's train was late on Monday and Tuesday.
b) She is going to France, Belgium, Spain and Italy in the summer.
c) He comes from Leeds and says it's great there.

4 **a) i)** False, **ii)** True, **iii)** False, **iv)** False, **v)** False, **vi)** False, **vii)** True

5 A logical argument would be that if racehorses are frequently injured in a particular race, eg one with difficult jumps, then it should not be held. It is not logical to compare racehorses with foxes. The value of the animal is irrelevant if you are assessing cruelty. Darren's argument is entirely different and unrelated to Nikki's. Whether or not fox hunting legislation is effective has no bearing on the danger (or otherwise) to racehorses. Finally, famine is a separate issue altogether. You cannot logically 'rank' problems in the world to find a top one and ignore the others until this is solved!

Accessing website links

Links to various websites are referred to throughout this BTEC Level 2 First Study Skills Guide. In order to ensure that these links are up to date, that they work and that the sites aren't inadvertently linked to any material that could be considered offensive, we have made the links available on our website: www.pearsonhotlinks.co.uk. When you visit the site, please enter the express code 5780S to gain access to the website links and information on how they can be used to help you with your studies.

Useful terms

Apprenticeships
Schemes that enable you to work and earn money at the same time as you gain further qualifications (an NVQ award and a technical certificate) and improve your functional skills. Apprentices learn work-based skills relevant to their job role and their chosen industry. Go to www.pearsonhotlinks.co.uk, insert the express code 5780S and click on the link for this useful term to find out more.

Assessment methods
Methods, such as practical tasks and assignments, which are used to check that your work demonstrates the learning and understanding you need to obtain the qualification.

Assessor
The tutor who marks or assesses your work.

Assignment
A complete task or mini-**project** set to meet specific grading criteria.

Assignment brief
The information and instructions related to a particular assignment.

BTEC Level 3 Nationals
Qualifications you can take when you have successfully achieved a Level 2 qualification, such as BTEC First. They are offered in a variety of subjects.

Credit value
The number of credits attached to your BTEC course. The credit value increases relative to the length of time you need to complete the course, from 15 credits for a BTEC Certificate, to 30 credits for a BTEC Extended Certificate and 60 credits for a BTEC Diploma.

Command word
The word in an assignment that tells you what you have to do to produce the type of answer that is required, eg 'list', 'describe', 'analyse'.

Educational Maintenance Award (EMA)
This is a means-tested award which provides eligible learners under 19, who are studying a full-time course at a centre, with a cash sum of money every week. Go to www.pearsonhotlinks.co.uk, insert the express code 5780S and click on the link for this useful term to find out more.

Functional skills
The practical skills that enable all learners to use and apply English, Maths and ICT both at work and in their everyday lives. They aren't compulsory to achieve on the course, but are of great use to you.

Grade
The rating of pass, merit or distinction that is given to an assignment you have completed, which identifies the standard you have achieved.

Grading criteria
The standard you have to demonstrate to obtain a particular grade in the unit. In other words, what you have to prove you can do.

Grading grid
The table in each unit of your BTEC qualification specification that sets out the grading criteria.

Indicative reading
Recommended books, magazines, journals and websites whose content is both suitable and relevant to the unit.

Induction
A short programme of events at the start of a course or work placement designed to give you essential information and introduce you to other people so that you can settle in easily.

Internal verification
The quality checks carried out by nominated tutors at all centres to ensure that all assignments are at the right level and cover appropriate learning outcomes. The checks also ensure that all **assessors** are marking work consistently and to the same standards.

Learning outcomes
The learning and skills you must demonstrate to show that you have learned a unit effectively.

Levels of study
The depth, breadth and complexity of knowledge, understanding and skills required to achieve a qualification determines its level. Level 2 is equivalent to GCSE level (grades A* to C). Level 3 equates to GCE A-level. As you successfully achieve one level, you can progress on to the next. BTEC qualifications are offered at Entry Level, then Levels 1, 2, 3, 4, 5, 6 and 7.

Mandatory units
On a BTEC Level 2 First course, these are the compulsory units that all learners must complete to gain the qualification.

Optional units
Units on your course from which you may be able to make a choice. They help you specialise your skills, knowledge and understanding and may help progression into work or further education.

Personal, learning and thinking skills (PLTS)
The skills and qualities that improve your ability to work independently and be more effective and confident at work. Opportunities for developing these are a feature of all BTEC First courses. They aren't compulsory to achieve on the course, but are of great use to you.

Plagiarism
Copying someone else's work or work from any other sources (eg the internet) and passing it off as your own. It is strictly forbidden on all courses.

Portfolio
A collection of work compiled by a learner – for an **assessor** – usually as evidence of learning.

Project
A comprehensive piece of work which normally involves original research and planning and investigation either by an individual or a team. The outcome will vary depending upon the type of project undertaken. For example, it may result in the organisation of a specific event, a demonstration of a skill, a presentation or a piece of writing.

Tutorial
An individual or small group meeting with your tutor at which you discuss the work you are currently doing and other more general course issues.

Unit content
Details about the topics covered by the unit and the knowledge and skills you need to complete it.

Work placement
Time spent on an employer's premises when you carry out work-based tasks as an employee and also learn about the enterprise to develop your skills and knowledge.

Work-related qualification
A qualification designed to help you to develop the knowledge and understanding you need for a particular area of work.